Traditional Recipes for

Pregnancy & Motherhood

Includes 80 Recipes from across India and 6 Superfoods

Sonal Chowdhary & Supriya Arun

JAICO PUBLISHING HOUSE
Ahmedabad Bangalore Bhopal Bhubaneswar Chennai
Delhi Hyderabad Kolkata Lucknow Mumbai

Published by Jaico Publishing House
A-2 Jash Chambers, 7-A Sir Phirozshah Mehta Road
Fort, Mumbai - 400 001
jaicopub@jaicobooks.com
www.jaicobooks.com

TRADITIONAL RECIPES FOR PREGNANCY & MOTHERHOOD
ISBN 978-93-86867-94-0

First Jaico Impression: 2018

Page design and layout:
Dhaivat Chhaya, Special Effects Graphics Design Company, Mumbai

Printed by
Print Plus Pvt. Ltd.
122, Shah & Nahar Ind. Estate (A-2),
Dhanraj Mills Compound, S. J. Marg,
Lower Parel (W), Mumbai – 400 013.

This book brings out the essence of Indian diversity and food wisdom. It is a one-of-its-kind book which offers scientifically-based nutritional rationales that will help pregnant and nursing mothers to make informed choices. It has a variety of interesting recipes to offer and you will learn about the usefulness of various herbs and plants and how to incorporate them in your everyday cooking.

Dr. Ashish Contractor
Head of Department of Rehabilitation and Sports Medicine at Sir H.N. Reliance Foundation Hospital & Author of The Heart Truth

Pregnancy is an important and beautiful phase of a woman's journey of life. Indian culture and traditional foods for this phase are very rich and a scientifically complete form of nutrition. Being a nutritionist and a mother myself, I value it thoroughly. To every woman out there, this is a book that beautifully merges nutritional science with tradition and I highly recommend it.

Kinita Kadakia Patel
An Award-winning Sports Nutritionist, Founder of Meal Pyramid & Author of The Athlete in You

The food of our grandmothers is the food of the gods. To nurture another, you must first nourish yourself. This book makes that easy. A must-have for every working woman.

Rashmi Bansal
Bestselling Author

Finally a book which caters to the Indian palate and sensibilities as well as keeps in mind the special needs of a pregnant woman. Just what the doctor ordered!

Dr. Rajeev Agarwal
Director, Care IVF

Inundated with information galore, the perinatal period seems to be more of a confusion than any clarity or peace. And here is a book in black and white that will be a true relish. Backed with research, well-explained ingredients, easy-to-make recipes and varieties from across the country, it sure is a must-have for a pregnant woman and a new mother. Simple, easy to read and an interesting book. Well recommended!

Rekha Sudarsan
Renowned Lactation Consultant, Psychologist, Childbirth Educator & Perinatal Fitness Expert

We all know that what we eat is important. But especially true for a mother to be. This book is a sincere effort from two of my most diligent students, Sonal and Supriya. It's an awesome collection of intelligent and appetizing recipes.

Dr. Vishwanath Prabhu
Life Care Consultant, ACSM, ACE & Reebok Faculty

Dedicated to our moms and grandmoms

CONTENTS

INTRODUCTION (1)

PREGNANCY AND MOTHERHOOD (3)

High-risk Pregnancy 5
Nutrition and Pregnancy 7
Lactation 13

SUPERFOODS FOR PREGNANCY AND LACTATION

Fenugreek 20
Garlic 22
Shatavari 24
Moringa 26
Gond (Gum Ghatti/Indian Edible Gum) 28
Turkey Berry (Sundakkai, Thai Brinjal) 30

TRADITIONAL REGIONAL RECIPES OF INDIA (33)

TAMIL NADU

Legiyam Podi (Post-childbirth Herb Powder) 39
Poondu Halwa (Garlic Halwa) 41
Angaya Podi (Dry Chutney Powder) 43
Suraa Puttu (Scrambled White Shark Fish) 45
Kandathippili Rasam (Long Pepper Soup) 47
Sirukkerai Masiyal (Tropical Amaranth Curry) 49

GUJARAT

Raab (Drink) 53
Ghaun No Sheero (Wheat Flour Halwa) 53
Methi Ane Khus Na Laadu (Fenugreek and Poppy Seed Ladoo) 55
Digestive Munch 56
Mouth Freshener 56
Special Tea 57
Flavored Drinking Water 57
Bajra No Sheero (Pearl Millet Halwa) 59

PUNJAB & HIMACHAL PRADESH

Khairani (Dry Fruits in Milk Base) 63
Moong Dal Halwa (Split Green Gram Halwa) 65
Seera (Germinated Wheat Fudge) 67

MAHARASHTRA

Methichi Kheer (Fenugreek Seed Pudding) 71
Khaskhaschi Kheer (Poppy Seed Pudding) 71
Alivche Ladoo (Garden Cress Seed Ladoos) 73
Khobra-Lahsunchi Chutney (Coconut-Garlic Chutney) 75
Lahsun-Tilachi Chutney (Garlic-Sesame Chutney) 75

KARNATAKA

Jeera Neeru (Black Cumin Tea) 79
Ragi Kanji (Finger Millet Porridge) 79
Sooji Kanji (Semolina Porridge) 81
Sunthi Kanji (Dry Ginger Porridge) 81
Vaali Ambat (Malabar Spinach Curry) 83
Sabsige Soppu Bhaat (Dill Leaves Rice) 85
Sabsige Soppu Saaru (Dill Leaves Soup) 87

RAJASTHAN

Gond Ke Ladoo (Edible Gum Ladoo) 91
Sauth Ki Moi (Dry Ginger and Wheat Mix) 93
Geeli Haldi (Wet Turmeric) 93
Haldi Ladoo (Turmeric Ladoo) 95
Kankari Ajwain (Carrom Seeds Mix) 97
Supari Ladoo (Areca Nut Ladoo) 99
Dashmool Kada (Herbal Decoction) 101
Battissa Kada (Herbal Decoction) 103
Laud Ladoo 105
Pipramul Milk 107
Khaskhas Ladoo (Poppy Seed Ladoo) 109
Paan Masala (Herbs with Betel Leaves) 111

BENGAL, ODISHA & NORTHEASTERN STATES

Shukto (Mixed Vegetable in Poppy Seed Paste) 115
Rui Macher Jhol (Rui Fish in Gravy) 117
Mochar Ghonto (Banana Flower and Potato) 119
Sabudana Kheer (Tapioca Pearl Pudding) 121
Muri Ladoo (Puffed Rice Ladoo) 121

UTTAR PRADESH

Suthora (Fox Nut and Dry Fruit Ladoos) 125
Harira (Mixed Nuts Snack) 127
Makhana Kheer (Fox Nut and Milk Pudding) 129
Ajwain Water (Carrom Seed Water) 129
Buknoo Churan (Digestive Herb Mix) 131

KERALA

Manga Chammandi (Raw Mango Chutney) 135
Muringaila Curry (Drumstick Leaf Curry) 137
Thengin Pookkula Lehyam
(Tender Coconut Flower Halwa) 139
Uluva Lehyam (Methi Halwa) 141

WHERE TRADITION MEETS SCIENCE AND CONVENIENCE (143)

SAMPLE DIET DURING PREGNANCY

2000kcal Vegetarian 144

2000kcal Non-vegetarian 145

SAMPLE DIET FOR POSTPARTUM

2350kcal Vegetarian 146

2350kcal Non-vegetarian 147

RECIPE IDEAS for pregnant women and HEALTHY SNACK IDEAS for lactating mothers

Manathakkali Keerai Kootu (Sunberry Leaf Dal) 151

Pan-roasted Chivda 153

Sundakkai Kadalai Kozhambu (Turkey Berry and Chickpeas in Gravy) 155

Millet Methi Pulao 157

Cheese Omelette Toast 159

Kanji Vada (Green Gram Fritters in Broth) 161

Fermented Rice Drink 163

Ragi Dosa with Vegetable Kurma 165

Aloo Poshto (Potatoes in Poppy Seed Gravy) 167

Methi Thepla (Fenugreek Leaf Flatbread) 169

Almond Sesame Chikki 171

Lotus Stem Pepper Fry 173

Halim Oats Relish Balls 175

Green Smoothie 177

Sattu Drink 177

Nuts and Seeds Energy Bar 179

Peanut/Kabuli Channa Sundal 181

Savoury Seed Mix 183

Antioxidant Trail Mix 183

A WORD ABOUT THE RECIPES (184)

SOME TIPS (184)

CONCLUSION (185)

ABOUT THE AUTHORS (186)

ACKNOWLEDGEMENTS (188)

BIBLIOGRAPHY (189)

Pregnancy is a crucial period in a woman's life. During this phase, it is of utmost importance to provide the best nourishment to the mother and her baby. One of the greatest gifts a mother can give her child is the gift of good health. During lactation, a wholesome and balanced diet is vital — for the mother's recovery as well as for the health of her newborn. So if you are a new mother or going to be one, this book will help you prepare for your wholesome journey to motherhood.

There are many misconceptions among the millennial generation regarding the customary pregnancy diet of our ancestors. As an alternative, new mothers/parents are drawn to Western food and lifestyle choices, mainly because there is little to no awareness about the positives and negatives of our traditional fare. Yes, there are negatives too, so there is no need to follow customs blindly. This book is an attempt to get you acquainted with the richness and wisdom of the traditional Indian diet and at the same time lay down an ideal pregnancy and post-pregnancy diet.

Food habits of various regions in India have been evolved over the years based on the climate, availability of foods and the genetic pool of the population in those areas. Regional diets contain a wealth of therapeutic and nutritional ingredients. To quote a research paper in the International Journal of Pharmacy and Pharmaceutical Science, "Many of the herbs used in postpartum care in a traditional way are rich in phenolic compounds and so found to be beneficial as powerful antioxidants."

With globalization and technological advancements we are forgetting the importance of our own foods that form the very base of our food ecosystem. It's true that with today's fast-paced life and

INTRODUCTION

nuclear family units, it is not possible to indulge in elaborate, traditional cooking routines. But the essence of these time-honored practices can be attained — just by following the steps given in this book and using the suggested ingredients with high nutritional value. The recipes in Part 3 of this book are all about striking that fine balance between nutrition and convenience.

According to Food Safety and Standards Authority of India (FSSAI), "currently there is no one place where information on India's rich food traditions, heritage and customs can be sought." As the country faces the loss of its diverse culinary heritage and micro-cuisines, FSSAI has decided to act by creating a repository offering cultural context, nutritional and even pharmaceutical values of Indian cuisines. This book is a small step in that direction. It is a compilation of all the wonderful region-wise recipes that have been passed down through generations.

We have tried to provide relevance and scientific basis to the recipes inside these pages, along with the benefits and uses of various herbs used during pregnancy and lactation; these preparations are rich in various macro- and micronutrients. Through this book, we aim to dispel pregnancy food-related myths. To make the reading experience more intimate, there are real-life pregnancy stories from various states, stories of women you can easily relate to, no matter what region you are from. This book is a ready reckoner for women looking for a nutritious meal plan that captures the richness of our timeless tradition; a journey that takes you back to the healing, nurturing nature and the legacy of traditional Indian cuisine.

Pregnancy begins with the conception or fertilization of the egg and continues until the delivery of the baby. It can be called as a collaboration between the mother, the foetus and the placenta to sustain and nurture a life.

Bearing a child is a transformative stage in a woman's life. Everything she eats, does or even thinks may have an effect on the development of the new life inside her. Each woman's pregnancy is different. In fact, even different pregnancies in the same woman usually vary. A mother who had severe morning sickness during her first pregnancy may have a breezy second one. However, certain physical and emotional changes and needs experienced by the expectant mothers are similar.

Pregnancy is generally divided into three trimesters or three periods of three months each. Most women experience the same general changes during each trimester.

PREGNANCY AND MOTHERHOOD

1st Trimester

For many women, a missed menstrual cycle is the first sign of pregnancy. Although, some women have very light periods for the first two months. The body produces high levels of estrogen and progesterone hormones to maintain the uterine lining, which in turn nourishes the foetus.

About half the women experience nausea and may vomit during early pregnancy, and sometimes even till the end. Though it can occur during any part of the day, it is called 'morning sickness'. Morning sickness is attributed to an increase in hormone levels, Vitamin B6 deficiency and/or low blood sugar.

In addition to this, some women also have indigestion and heartburn issues. The hormones relaxin and progesterone cause the food to be retained in the stomach for a long time, causing heartburn and intestinal muscle relaxation leading to constipation. Another reason for heartburn is the unassimilated iron supplement. This can be prevented by having a Vitamin C source like orange juice along with the iron supplement.

Fatigue is a common feature during this trimester.

2nd Trimester

The second trimester - 15th to 28th week - is often the most enjoyable of the 40 weeks. The fatigue and nausea is a thing of the past; the pregnancy becomes visible to all. Though the body of the pregnant woman becomes big considerably, it is not big enough to make daily activities. The mother can perceive the child's movements between 16 to 18 weeks. By the end of this trimester, blood volume and stroke volume in the mother will increase by 40% to 60%. Edema in pregnant women is common due to increased blood volume. Pregnancy-induced hypertension surfaces during this period.

3rd Trimester

The third trimester or the last three months is the time for preparing for the birth of the baby physically, mentally and emotionally. A major physical change is the rapid increase in the uterus size reaching up to 11 to 14 inches. The growing uterus puts pressure on the stomach and intestines pushing them up and back causing a burning sensation, constipation and shortness of breath. Carrying the increased weight can lead to a return of the fatigue aspect in this trimester.

Fun Fact: By nine months, the pregnant uterus expands to 500 times its original size. That's about the equivalent of a medium-sized pear growing to a medium size watermelon!

High-risk Pregnancy

Some pregnant women are considered to be at a higher risk than others if they have diabetes, thyroid issues, heart disease or high blood pressure, or those who develop these conditions during pregnancy or labour.

They also include women who are under 17 or over 35 years, or carrying their fifth or later child, or carrying more than one baby.

Women who start developing signs of pre-term labour are known to be at a higher risk than normal.

The risk degree, of course, varies on a case-to-case basis.

Gestational Diabetes

Diabetes or higher-than-normal blood sugar occurring during the course of pregnancy is called gestational diabetes. Pregnancy increases the insulin resistance, or in other words, the insulin a pregnant woman produces is less effective in bringing the glucose under control. The resultant high blood sugar levels can cause complications in the pregnant woman and the foetus. This condition disappears after childbirth, though the woman remains at a danger of acquiring gestational diabetes during any subsequent pregnancies also.

The common factors in women developing gestational diabetes are obesity, lurking insulin resistance before conceiving and pregnancy after 25. Therefore, all pregnant women are routinely screened for blood sugar levels. Untreated diabetic women may conceive a very large baby making delivery very difficult. There is also a danger of the newborn becoming hypoglycemic as soon as he is born and so has to be breastfed immediately. Women who have diabetes are more likely to develop pregnancy-induced hypertension.

Pregnancy-induced Hypertension

Most women who have hypertension during pregnancy did not have it before and will not have it after. Some studies suggest that it occurs due to the imbalance created in the blood vessel constriction and dilatation due to the altered hormonal environment. The reason could be hereditary, a diet low in protein and calcium, chronic high blood pressure, age, multiple pregnancy and concurrent diabetes. Several studies prove that a good diet with the right protein and calcium level can reduce the risk of pregnancy-induced hypertension.

High blood pressure affects both the mother and the child. A high resistance in the blood vessels supplying the uterus can decrease the blood flow and oxygen supply to the foetus affecting its growth. If the blood pressure is uncontrollable, labour may have to be induced to stop further damage.

Multiple Pregnancy

If a woman is pregnant with more than one baby, say with twins, triplets or more, then the demands placed on the woman's body increases tenfold. The uterus is larger, the demand from the circulatory system is more and the nutritional requirements increased. The protein intake has to be upped in order to support the growth of the babies and to increase the muscle strength of the uterus.

Nutrition and Pregnancy

The healthy tissues of the body are dependent on the nutritional aspects of a person's diet. This fact becomes even more significant for a woman during the journey of pregnancy when a human body with all the tissue differentiation is created. The entire growth of the baby inside the womb and (after the birth) while being breastfed is dependent on the mother's nourishment. The baby's heart, liver, bones, brain are all formed completely from the nutrients the mother's body provides. There can't be a more emphatic statement than this to drive home how important it is to meet the mother's nutritional requirements.

A poor diet can cause a plethora of issues for a woman, including anaemia, infection, placental malfunction, difficult labour and failure at breastfeeding. The baby can suffer prematurity, low birth weight or even stillbirth. However, pregnancy is not the licence to gorge on calories. Empty calories must be replaced by a balanced diet with a special emphasis on good quality protein intake.

Some women start paying attention to their diet on becoming pregnant as they desire to do everything right to yield a healthy baby. Some on the other hand start getting concerned about their subsequent weight gain.

Is there any optimal weight gain? The amount of weight gained varies from woman to woman as does the pattern of weight gain. Total weight gain during pregnancy is determined with the help of pre-pregnancy weight, eating habits, metabolism and daily activities. However, if a woman was underweight before becoming pregnant, she will need to gain more weight than an average woman.

Important considerations in each case are the quantity and quality of weight gain.

Approximately 1 to 2 kgs is the average amount of weight gain that occurs during the first trimester of pregnancy. Thereafter, approximately 0.5 kg per week during the remainder of the pregnancy is typical, although there are exceptions. If there is abnormally steep weight gain after twentieth week of pregnancy, which may indicate abnormal water retention, it must be looked into. Inversely, low maternal weight gain during the second or third trimester increases the risk of intrauterine growth restriction, which must be watched too.

The weight increase in the second trimester with respect to the first is strongly correlated to the infant's length at birth. The consequences of low weight gain are low birth weight of the baby, early birth as well as life-long problems for the baby. If there is too much weight gain, due to the baby's size and pelvic size disproportion, birth can be difficult. Gestational diabetes is also a risk.

Is there any calorie recommendation?
An average increase of 340kcals/day during the second trimester of pregnancy and approximately 450kcals in the third trimester. However, this is calculated based on the pre-pregnancy weight. So the

total calorie recommendation comes to about 2200 to 2800kcals/day for a normal weight woman, which is an increase of about 15% to 20% over the energy needs of a non-pregnant woman.

An average fruit is around 50 to 75kcals, so getting that extra 340 calories doesn't take a lot of food. What is important is how the extra calories cater to the specific requirements of pregnancy.

The weight gain goal based on per-pregnancy weight:

Pre-pregnancy Weight	Weight Gain Goal
Underweight women (BMI of < 18.5kg/m^2)	28-40lb or 12.7 to 18kg
Normal weight women (BMI of 18.5 to 24.9kg/m^2)	25 to 35lb or 11.4 to 15.9kg
Overweight women (BMI of 25 to 29.9kg/m^2)	15-25lb or 6.8 to 11.4kg
Obese women (BMI of > 30k/m^2)	11 to 20lb or 5 to 9 kg
Women who are carrying twins or triplets	25 to 54lb or 11.4 to 24.5kg
Teenage girls	35 to 40lb or 15.9 to 18kg

Protein

Why is protein important?

According to the recommendations of the Nutrition Society of India, the protein requirement of a sedentary woman is 0.8 to 1.0 g/kg of the original body weight. During pregnancy, the 'additional' protein requirement is 0.3 g/ kg of body weight over and above the normal requirement. This means as the pregnancy advances, the protein requirement also increases proportionally.

This is because protein serves as building blocks for the growth of the new tissues during pregnancy. The placenta, which is the connection between the foetus and the mother, requires protein for its complete development. It has to be sustained and nourished throughout the pregnancy.

The foetus grows from one cell to innumerable cells in only 9 months and such rapid growth demands high amounts of protein. There will also be an increase in the development of the uterine and breast tissues to support the foetus. The mother's blood volume increases by 50% during pregnancy. Plasma proteins and haemoglobin, two vital components of the blood, are proteins too. The amniotic fluid, which protects the foetus from shock and injury, contains a variety of proteins.

Ideally, the protein intake should be of 'high biologic value' and 'complete', which means they should be easily absorbed by the body and contain all the essential amino acids required by the body.

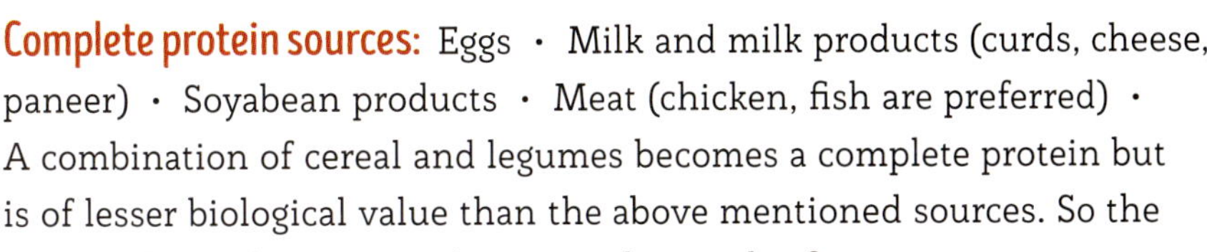

Complete protein sources: Eggs • Milk and milk products (curds, cheese, paneer) • Soyabean products • Meat (chicken, fish are preferred) • A combination of cereal and legumes becomes a complete protein but is of lesser biological value than the above mentioned sources. So the amount has to be increased to meet the needs of a pregnant woman.

Calcium

Pregnancy demands increased mineral and vitamin levels to meet the heightened metabolic activity in the mother. A good supply of calcium along with phosphorus, magnesium and Vitamin D is essential for the development of bones and teeth of the foetus along with the mother's wellbeing. One of the wonders of nature is that the body absorbs increased amounts of calcium and zinc directly from the food during the pregnancy period. Food sources of calcium and phosphorus are the same, so if the diet has enough calcium, phosphorus is also taken care of.

Calcium requirement: 1000mg/day

Supplementation recommended if the diet is calcium deficient.

Dietary Sources: Milk and milk products (Curds, cheese, paneer) • Fortified soybean products • Poppy, sesame, coriander and mustard seeds.

Iron

Iron is a very important mineral during pregnancy as it is essential for the haemoglobin synthesis due to an increase in mother's blood volume at this time. The baby also stores some iron in its body before the birth. Iron deficiency increases the chances of preterm birth and low birth weight babies. The amount of iron in the food is a poor predictor of iron uptake by the body as the direct absorption of iron is only 3% to 10%. Iron uptake can be improved by the intake of food items high in Vitamin C along with other dietary iron sources and avoiding foods that limit iron absorption like tea, coffee and unleavened whole grain breads because caffeine and high fibre food inhibit iron absorption. Caffeine intake inhibits the body's uptake of iron, calcium and zinc. It also passes into the breast milk, so caffeine consumption during lactation should be limited.

Iron requirement: 38mg/day

This amount is difficult to be met through diet alone so a supplement is prescribed.

Dietary Sources: **Haem iron** – fish, poultry, meat and organ meat
Non-haem iron – Cauliflower leaves, amaranth greens, radish leaves, Turkey berries, rice flakes (Poha), pearl millet (Bajra), roasted Bengal gram and garden cress seeds (Halim).

Zinc

Zinc is a mineral whose requirement increases as the pregnancy progresses. It plays a role in the synthesis of nucleic acids RNA and DNA. Zinc deficiency leads to obstetric complications and congenital malformation in the foetus. Non-vegetarian sources are rich in zinc; vegetarians may require supplementation.

Zn

Zinc requirement per day: First trimester - 5.5mg
Second trimester - 7mg | Third trimester - 10mg | Lactation - 9.5mg

Dietary Sources: Meat · Nuts and seeds · Wheat germ · Oats · lentils

Vitamin C, D, Beta-carotene, Retinol

Vitamin A and C are required in higher amounts due to their role in tissue growth. While Vitamin C aids in formation of connective tissue and vascular functioning along with aiding iron absorption, Vitamin A is essential for normal vision in the baby, epidermal skin formation and gene transcription. Beta-carotene and retinol are precursors for vitamin A and found in some food sources.

Vitamin D ensures absorption and use of calcium and phosphorus for the fetal bone growth. Mother's exposure to sunlight also increases her endogenous synthesis of Vitamin D. Even with abundant sunlight, many Indian women have Vitamin D deficiency. Lactose intolerant vegetarian or vegan mothers can get their dietary inputs from fortified soy milk.

Vitamin C requirement:
In pregnancy 40mg/day | During lactation 80mg/day

Dietary Sources: Indian gooseberry (Amla), citrus fruits, guava, tomatoes, strawberries, potatoes, broccoli, leafy greens.

Vitamin D requirement: 10mcg/day or 400IU/day

Dietary Sources: Milk, cheese, fortified dairy products, fortified soymilk, fish, egg yolks.

Beta -carotene requirement: 2400mcg/day (veg source)

Dietary Sources: Dark green leafy vegetables (agathi greens has the highest amount), carrot, broccoli, spinach, butter/ghee, cheese, sweet potato.

Retinol requirement: 600mcg/day (animal source)

Dietary Sources: Egg yolk, beef liver, chicken breast, fish.

Folic Acid

One of the most important requirements for normal foetal development is folic acid or folate, especially in the initial days of conception. It is so important that doctors suggest to a woman who is planning to conceive that she start taking folic acid supplements even before she becomes pregnant, since it has a role even before the pregnancy comes to light. It helps in cell division and nucleotide synthesis. Inadequate levels can cause neural tube defects and congenital heart diseases. The neural tube forms during the critical period of 17 days to 30 days of gestation and it grows to be the spinal cord of the baby. Folate also builds mature red blood cells throughout the pregnancy.

A study has demonstrated that the average loss of folates during Indian style of cooking is 33% and average density of folates in Indian meal is about 50mcg/1000 kcals, It is assumed that at least 50% of folate present in the diet is absorbed.

The actual requirement of free folic acid ranges between 50-100mcg depending on the age. However, during pregnancy and lactation, the requirement increases.

B9

Folic acid requirement:
400mcg/day in pregnancy | 150mcg/day in lactation

Dietary Sources: Sheep/goat liver, eggs, bengal gram, amaranth leaves, cluster beans, sesame seeds, ladies finger, black gram, red gram, cow peas (chowli), soya bean, oatmeal, green leafy vegetables.

Vitamin B12

Like folic acid, vitamin B12 is also involved in the maturation of cells, so its deficiency causes megaloblastic anaemia. This vitamin is also required for the metabolism of folic acid.

Vitamin B12 is synthesized by bacteria and is present only in animal foods.

Although a majority of Indians live on a vegetarian diet, vitamin B12 deficiency as such is not widespread. The reason could be the intake of milk products, fermented food preparations as well as polluted environment and unhygienic eating practices.

B12

Vitamin B12 requirement:
Pregnancy 1.2mcg/day | Lactation 1.5mcg/day

Dietary Sources: For vegetarians: Milk, curd, cheese and skimmed milk powder, fermented foods. For non-vegetarians: Shrimp, buffalo and goat meat, eggs, goat and sheep liver.

Lactation

The World Health Organization states that breastfeeding is "an unequalled way of providing ideal food for the healthy growth and development of the infants." Breastfeeding is recommended as the exclusive source of nutrition for the infants who are up to six months old. After six months, iron-fortified complementary foods should be added to the basic diet of breast milk.

Breast milk is nutritionally superior to any other alternative. Breastfeeding has immense benefits for both the mother and the baby. It promotes a close mother-child bond. For the mother, breastfeeding reduces stress, prevents postpartum depression and Type 2 diabetes. It also protects against breast and ovarian cancer. Plus it helps the mother to shed the pregnancy weight.

The benefits for the baby is that it decreases the risk of sudden infant death syndrome, Type 1 and 2 diabetes, leukemia, Hodgkin's disease, obesity, hypercholesterolemia and asthma. It lowers the risk of allergies as the breast milk contains certain anti-infectious factors and immunological substances which strengthen the baby's immune system. Breast milk is bacteriologically safe and always fresh and babies are less likely to be overfed this way.

The initial breast milk that comes out is known as colostrum. It is a thin yellow fluid that is rich in proteins and antibodies. It makes the immune system and the digestive health of the baby strong. So it's very important for the baby to get sufficient breast milk. That is why a sound nutritional diet ensures good milk production in the mother. When there is no milk production post-delivery, it is termed as Agalactia.

After the birth of the baby, women experience a rapid drop in the circulating levels of estrogen and progesterone accompanied by a rapid increase in the hormone prolactin secretion, setting the stage for copious milk supply. The usual stimulus for milk production and secretion is suckling. Oxytocin, the milk-releasing hormone, can be released by touch, smell, visual and auditory stimuli as well as thinking about the infant. Adrenalin release is supposed to negate the effects of oxytocin. That is why stress can be a big factor in reducing the milk secretion.

There are many causes of breast milk insufficiency:

- Nutritional deficiencies
- Hormonal imbalance
- Weakness
- Prolonged labour with excessive postnatal loss of blood and fluids
- Blocked milk ducts
- Stress, fatigue & insomnia
- Insulin resistance
- Hypothyroidism

For normal breast milk production one should stick to a healthy diet, drink sufficient fluids, reduce stress and sleep well.

Nutritional Requirements of Lactation

Lactation is nutritionally very demanding, especially for a mother who nurses her infant exclusively for several months. Increased intake of most of the nutrients is advised. Milk production is most affected by the frequency of suckling and maternal hydration. However, milk composition varies according to the mother's diet. For example, the fatty acid composition of a mother's milk reflects her dietary intake. The breast milk's concentration of micronutrients like selenium, iodine and some water soluble B-vitamins are also reflective of the mother's diet. Lower levels of these nutrients in the milk is a sign of an undernourished mother.

Production of 100ml of milk requires an 85kcals expenditure of energy by the mother. During the first six months of lactation, the average milk production is 750ml/day (around 600kcals energy of the mother) with a range of about 550ml/day to 1200ml/day. Infants who suckle and feed well stimulate better volume of milk.

The recommended dietary allowance for the first six months is an addition of only 350kcals/day over the pre-pregnancy recommended calorie intake. For the next six months, a 400kcals/day above the pre-pregnancy level is advised. The rest of the energy for the milk production comes from the maternal fat stores. In case of mothers who have gained a lot of weight during pregnancy, not more than 200kcals/day extra is recommended. As a general rule, a calorie intake of at least 1800kcals is recommended in the first six months of the lactation period.

Dietary Requirements per Day

Nutrient	Requirement
Protein	1.2g/kg of current weight
Carbohydrates	160 to 210g
Fats	10mcg/day or 400IU/day
DHA Omega 3	200mg
Calcium	1200mg
Vitamin D	15mcg/day or 600IU/day
Zinc	14mg
Iron	25mg

There are certain foods that are believed to increase lactation and mostly these are the foods that are added in the traditional recipes. They are named "Galactogogues".

Oats, barley, fenugreek, shatavari, fennel seeds, gum resin from axle wood tree (gond), dates, poppy seeds, garden cress seeds, pumpkin seeds, melon seeds, jaggery, ajwain, dry ginger powder and tapioca pearls (sabudana) are some of the popular ingredients in the food prepared for the lactating mother in India.

Certain medical conditions of the mother can affect the breast milk production. The most common are insulin resistance and hypothyroidism. A landmark study published in the *Advances in Nutrition*, 2016, by Dr. Laurie Nommsen-Rivers establishes a link between the suboptimal glucose metabolism (as in the case of insulin resistance, late pregnancy and sometimes thyroid) with inadequate lactation.

She in her research propounds that the 'PTPRF' gene as the biomarker for breastfeeding problems. This gene is supposed to suppress signals among cells that are usually triggered by insulin binding to its receptor on the cell surface. The mother has to be careful about her carbohydrates (especially simple sugars) in her diet in these cases.

Another instance where the mother influences the infant's feed is when the former suffers from the 'leaky gut syndrome', an autoimmune condition. The colon is compromised, which leads to undigested food substances in the blood and therefore in the breast milk, which can cause indigestion in the feeding infant. Identification of the allergen and avoiding it becomes important in such cases.

Lactation and Galactagogues

The human mammary glands develop in stages.

Stage 1 or **Lactogenesis 1** is when the mammary glands develop extensively during pregnancy but secretion is withheld by the high circulating levels of progesterone.

Stage 2 or **Lactogenesis 2** takes place after delivery (30-40 hours later) of a full-term infant. When the placenta is expelled, the progesterone levels drop, the levels of hormone prolactin are increased which trigger the milk production.

Stage 3 or **Galactopoiesis** is from day 9 post-partum until the mother decides to wean.

Stage 4 or **Involution** is when the breast stop producing milk completely.

Oxytocin is a hormone required for the removal of the milk from the breast by the squeezing of the ducts. Its level are increased by sensory stimulation like a crying infant or the suckling of the infant.

Insulin is also important in Stage 2 as it makes the nutrients more available for milk synthesis.

Thyroid hormone appears to be necessary for mammary responsiveness to growth hormone and prolactin during lactation.

Social and psychological factors also strongly influence a mother's ability to nurse. Other common causes of insufficient milk production include diabetes, obesity, polycystic ovarian syndrome (PCOS).

There are no specific diagnostic tests for lactation insufficiency. Maternal perception and low growth rate of the infant are valid indicators of Stage 2 insufficiency.

Other common reported reasons for unsuccessful breastfeeding or early weaning apart from perceived low milk supply is poor breastfeeding technique or latching leading to ineffectual milk removal, deficient mammary gland issue and maternal hormonal imbalances. Once these issues have been addressed, and other strategies like prepping of the mother by a lactation consultant are followed and still the milk supply is insufficient, safe herbal galactagogues could be tried.

Over the years herbs and foods have been used as galactagogues by women to maintain an increase milk supply. In the past, a good human milk supply for new-borns and infants was crucial for survival in the absence of any artificial substitutes like today. Historically it is evident that nations, cultures and tribes developed traditions based on the herbs and foods to maintain and increase milk supply. These herbs and foods are collectively called as galactagogues. These mainly act by stimulating the hormone called oxytocin. Common herbs and foods used as galactagogues are varied and include aniseed, asparagus, borage, caraway, chicken soup, coconut, coriander, cumin, fennel, fenugreek, garlic, ginger, millets, mushroom, oat straw, pumpkin, papaya, sesame seeds, sunflower seeds, goat's rue and milk thistle to name a few.

Herbal galactagogues are widely used in India, It is estimated that about 15% of breastfeeding women in the United States have used botanical galactagogues. In spite of its wide usage, there is a significant disconnect between usage and support from conventional health care practitioners.

In rural India and in families that

follow traditional practices, women embrace the 'just in case' approach to use these herbs that increase the milk supply prophylactically in order to avoid breast milk supply issues.

In a study documented in the *BMC Complementary and Alternative Medicine* 2014 issue, several women who were breastfeeding were interviewed to understand their perception of using herbals during lactation.

The underlying theme observed was the strong mental will of the women to breastfeed.

One woman commented, "I certainly am not opposed to the idea of using herbs to support breastfeeding. Really, I don't care what it is, as long as I can tolerate it and it helps. I am willing to try anything."

There seemed to be a relationship between the women's breastfeeding confidence level and the duration of exclusive breastfeeding. Even in the absence of milk volume measurement, one participant described how the use of herbal galactagogues promoted her confidence and fostered self-empowerment to breastfeed.

One participant just summed it all up...

"I think people need to know that it does actually work, not just some crazy hippy thing, because actually that was what I thought. I initially thought that the herbs were for people who didn't want to use conventional medicines because they have issues with pharma or whatever, but honestly for me, it has worked wonders, so I just wish that more women are aware of it."

As we went about researching and collecting information about the practices in the different regions of India, one thing that struck us was the commonality of some of the ingredients across cultures and regions. These ingredients are incorporated in their respective traditional diets for pregnant and lactating mothers in different ways and recipes for maintenance of well-being, prevention of anaemia and stimulation of milk production.

To corroborate the book's promise of providing a scientific bridge between the tradition and the modern, we decided to dig deep into some published research papers to see if any established scientific reasoning can be given to the usage. We found abundant supporting research, which we are happy to present to you in order to convince you about the reported uses and properties of the ingredients.

There are two types of people: ones who believe anything traditional is very good for health since our ancestors would have seen some reason before propagating it. The other type does not believe in the old practices until they are completely convinced about the scientific basis. The aim of this chapter is to satisfy and convince both these types by bringing to the fore the star ingredients along with the research to prove their actions. We encourage you to incorporate these ingredients freely in your diet to reap the benefits.

We chose six ingredients that are widely used and also supported by good research.

Moringa, fenugreek, shatavari and garlic are regulars in a postpartum diet and also proven galactagogues, while edible gum/gond (common in north India) and Turkey berry (common in south of the Vindhyas) are ingredients included to provide strength and improvement in the mother's health post-delivery.

Apart from these purposes, these ingredients were also found to possess myriad elements and their beneficial properties are documented. One of the common features among all the ingredients are their antioxidant properties.

Free radicals are highly reactive molecules or chemical species capable of independent existence. Molecular and cellular damage due to reactive oxygen species and reactive nitrogen species is widely believed to be the major cause of chronic degenerative diseases, including cardiovascular diseases and cancer. Antioxidants are of great interest because they help to protect the body against damage by reactive oxygen species (ROS).

In recent years there has been an increasing interest in finding antioxidant phytochemicals, because they can inhibit the propagation of free radical reactions and protect the human body from diseases. The most effective components seem to be flavonoids and phenolic compounds of many plant raw materials, particularly in herbs, seeds, and fruits. Their metal-chelating capabilities and radical-scavenging properties have enabled phenolic compounds to be thought of as effective free radical scavengers and inhibitors of lipid peroxidation. Vegetables and fruits are rich sources of antioxidants, such as vitamin A, C, E, carotenoids, polyphenolic compounds and flavonoids which prevent free radical damage reducing the risk of chronic diseases.

FENUGREEK

A valuable, multi-use ingredient

Fenugreek seeds (*Trigonella foenumgraecum*), our very own 'methi', is the most commonly used herbal galactagogues in published literature. It is an important ingredient in Indian curry powders. It enhances the flavour and modifies the colour and texture of the dishes.

Fenugreek seeds contain around 25% protein, 7% fat and 58% carbohydrates out of which 25% is dietary fibre. The antidiabetic and lipid-lowering uses of fenugreek are attributed to the high dietary fibre constituent. It is also used as a food stabiliser, adhesive and emulsifying agent due to its fibre, protein and gum content. It has a beneficial influence on digestion and constipation. Fenugreek is a rich source of iron, containing 33mg/100g dry weight.

The main chemical constituents are steroidal sapogenins, phytoestrogens and polyphenols. The phytoestrogens are are similar in chemical structure to the female hormone estrogen and can bind to the estrogen receptors in the body thus having an impact on the endocrine system. This could be the reason for its effect on lactation. It is also thought that fenugreek stimulates sweat production, and since the breast is a modified sweat gland, fenugreek may affect the breast milk production in this manner. Some scientists have reported that fenugreek can increase a nursing mother's milk supply within 24-72 hours after taking the herb. The polyphenols are well-known free radical scavengers aiding its use as a powerful antioxidant. Fenugreek extracts have been shown to be having antifungal and antibacterial action also.

Fenugreek is also known for its lymphatic cleansing activity through its vital role in removing toxic waste, dead cells and trapped proteins from the body. A block in lymphatic system can mean poor circulation of fluid, fluid retention, pain, energy loss and disease, anywhere in the body. Drinking water in which seeds of fenugreek are soaked helps in softening and dissolving the cellular masses.

The fenugreek leaves are rich in calcium, zinc, iron, phosphorus, carotene, B-Complex vitamins and high amounts of vitamin C.

Including fenugreek leaves and seeds in the everyday diet and adding germinated fenugreek powder at 5% to 10% levels to the wheat flour can increase the total protein, iron, zinc, calcium, vitamin B2, carotene, vitamin E and C content in the food.

A maternity unit in Ankara, Turkey, enrolled healthy women, with full-term infants willing to exclusively breastfeed in a study to find if fenugreek tea indeed helped in increased milk production. While one group drank herbal tea with 100mg of fenugreek seed powder the other placebo group was given apple tea with the same colour and look. The mean breast milk volume for the fenugreek group, the placebo group and the control group was 73.2 ml, 38.8 ml and 31.1 ml respectively. The researchers finally concluded that a herbal tea containing fenugreek enhanced the breast milk production and might be used to support exclusive breastfeeding.

So we can safely conclude that fenugreek seeds should be a sure shot ingredient in the diet of a new mother breastfeeding her infant.

Intake limit: One can safely take up to 30gm of seeds per day.

For fenugreek-based recipes, refer pages 55, 71, 141, 155, 157, 169.

GARLIC

Baby's favourite flavour

Over the centuries, different cultures have recognized the several uses of garlic with respect to different diseases. Garlic (*Allium sativum*) is considered a prophylactic as well as a therapeutic medicinal plant. Ancient Egyptians used garlic to treat diarrhoea and its medical prowess was inscribed in walls of the temples and on papyrus as far back as 1500 BC. *Zenda Avesta*, the holy writings of Zoroastrianism compiled during the 6th century BC, also mentions garlic and its uses. It is also believed that during the earliest Olympics in Greece, garlic was fed to the athletes for increasing their stamina.

Garlic contains at least 33 sulfur compounds (responsible for its pungent odour), several enzymes, minerals germanium, calcium, copper, iron, potassium, magnesium, selenium and zinc; vitamins A, B1 and C, fiber and water. It also contains 17 amino acids. One of the most biologically active compounds in garlic is 'allicin'. The most abundant sulfur compound in garlic is 'alliin', which is considered to have the antioxidant and free radical scavenging properties.

Garlic reduces high blood pressure. It helps prevent heart diseases by scavenging the free radicals, reducing cholesterol synthesis and increasing the microcirculation. It protects the neurons from neuro toxicity. Garlic constituents can reduce fibrin formation and thereby having an anticlotting effect. Studies have clearly shown that it suppresses the low density lipoprotein (LDL) formation and increases the resistance of LDL to oxidation. It has antibacterial, antifungal, and antiviral properties.

Garlic is another widely used condiment/flavour enhancer in the Indian diet. It so happens that the newborn baby too seems to prefer the flavour. Human milk provides the potential for a rich source of varying chemosensory experiences to the infant. It has been documented that when the mother's milk is supplemented with garlic flavour, the infants breastfeed longer than they do when garlic is absent in the mother's diet. The infant is attracted to or stimulated by the sulfur-based garlic volatiles, which in turn increases the suckling process. Prolonged suckling would in turn induce more oxytocin and as a result eject more milk. In fact, it has been said in a study that the infant's prior exposure to flavours in mother's milk could actually increase the desirability of those flavours through familiarization. Pregnant mothers can consume more garlic thereby possibly exposing the foetus to the flavour of garlic.

There is another study suggesting that there is a clear increase in the prolactin levels when the nursing mother consumes garlic galactagogues.

Intake limit: Up to 15gm of garlic can be consumed in a day. Garlic extracts in the form of capsules are not recommended. Garlic pods can be added to food preparations and consumed.

For garlic-heavy recipes, please refer to pages 41, 49, 75, 83, 119, 137, 157, 165, 173.

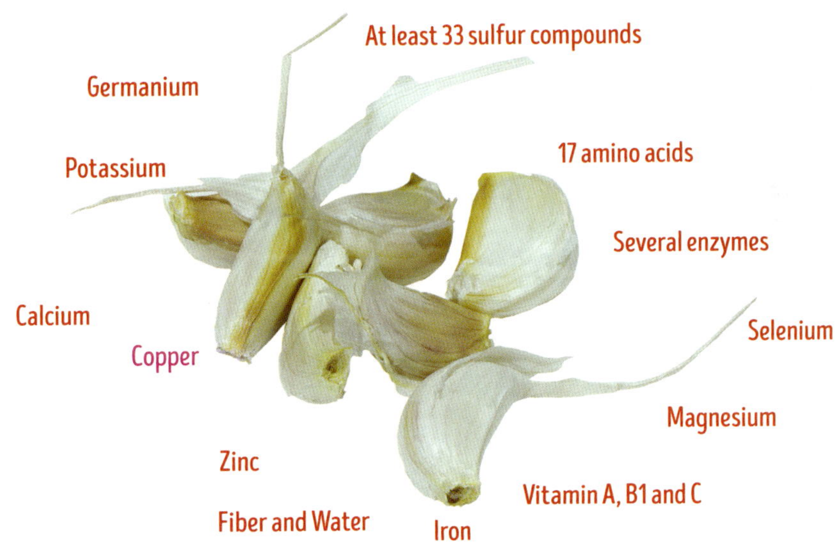

SHATAVARI

The prolactin inducer

Shatavari (*Asparagus racemosus*) is a tall, climbing, thorny undershrub with spiny branches and white flowers found in tropical regions of India, Australia and Africa. It has been prominently mentioned in Ayurvedic literature for the diuretic, antidysenteric, nutritive, galactagogue, aphrodisiac and antispasmodic properties of its roots. Its role as a galactagogue has been mentioned in several ancient Ayurvedic textbooks such as *Charak Samhita* and *Susruta Samhita*.

In Ayurveda, shatavari is considered a tonic for women. It is reported to be beneficial for female infertility, sexual organ inflammation and dryness. It helps in follicle genesis, ovulation, preparing the womb for conception and avoiding miscarriages. It acts as a postpartum tonic by increasing lactation and normalizing the uterus and changing hormones.

The chemical analysis of its roots revealed the presence of several pharmacologically active steroidal saponins named the 'shatavarins', a group of chemical entities known to be useful in various ways like an antioxidant, blood cholesterol reducer, anti-microbial, anti-protozoal, anti-cancer, hepato-protector.

A study involving 60 lactating women between 20 to 40 years of age feeding their less-than-six-months-old infants was conducted in the SVSP Hospital in Kolkata. The mothers had one or more of the symptoms, namely deficient lactation, painful sensation in the breast while feeding, infant crying just after feeding, loss of appetite in the mother or the manifestation of any anxiety disorder which could affect lactation.

The results of the clinical study showed that the oral administration of the shatavari herb had a definite positive impact on the primary parameter, the prolactin hormone level in the lactating mothers. The increase in the mean prolactin hormone level of the female subjects in the research group was three times more than that of the subjects of the control group during the study period. This is corroborated by the secondary outcomes, namely the increase in the weight of the mothers and weight of the babies in the research group compared to the control group. The subjective satisfaction of the mothers regarding the state of lactation and the well-being and happiness of the babies also showed manifold increase in the overall ratings over the duration of study in the research group subjects when compared to the control group.

The overall research findings corroborate and validate the galactagogue property of the research drug which has been ascribed to it in the ancient texts of India. Shatavari was also found to be quite safe from acute oral toxicity.

This should remove all kinds of doubts from the minds of mothers which deters them from using the herb though it is has been used for several centuries in India. Shatavari can be safely used as a galactagogue in cases of lactation inadequacy.

Intake limit: Aqueous extract of up to 2.5g/kg body weight has not showed any human toxicity.

Shatavari is included the recipes in pages 99, 101.

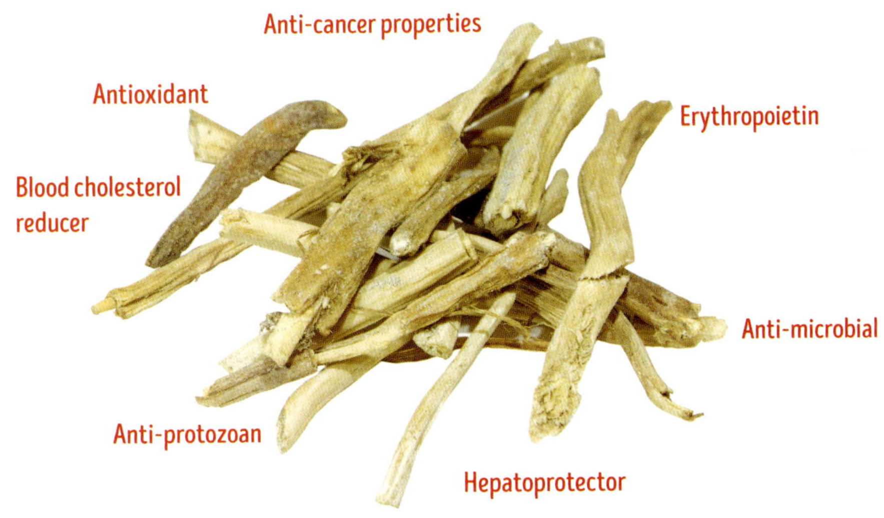

MORINGA

Mother's best friend

Moringa *oleifera* is one of the world's most useful trees. It is sometimes called the 'miracle tree' or 'Mother's best friend' as almost every part of the tree can be used for food, medication and industrial purposes. Different parts of the tree are endowed with different types of chemicals with useful biological functions. Some act as antioxidants in free-radical scavenging, relieving the body of oxidative stress and cancer. Others possess antibacterial, antiviral, antifungal, anti-inflammatory, antispasmodic and diuretic properties.

Moringa leaves have been reported to contain seven times the vitamin C of oranges, four times the calcium of milk, four times the vitamin A of carrots and three times the potassium of carrots. The leaves are highly nutritious and as such are recommended for nursing mothers especially those from developing countries or any area prone to malnutrition.

Moringa leaves are a source of complete and quality protein that can be equated to soybeans because it contains all the essential amino acids in the right proportion.

Moringa supports a healthy cardiovascular system, promotes normal blood-glucose levels, neutralizes free radicals that cause cancer, provides support for the body's anti-inflammatory mechanism, enriches the blood, and supports the immune system. It improves eyesight, mental alertness and bone strength. It has a potential role in dealing with malnutrition, general weakness, lactation problems, depression and osteoporosis.

Moringa is widely used as a herbal galactagogue in southern India and in the Philippines. Dr. E. Quisumbing was the first scientist to do a study on its lactogenic properties in 1987. Later studies have proved the causal relationship between moringa intake and increased milk production by demonstrating increased serum prolactin production in the anterior pituitary gland.

Pooling the results of several studies conducted on breastfeeding women, it can be concluded that moringa causes significant increase in breast milk volume by day seven. It also results in improvement in the infant's weight gain. The studies also showed that there was also a statistically significant increase in the mother's prolactin levels. Safety profile was merely obtained through self-report; no adverse event was seen in the six studies pooled.

Intake limits: Moringa leaf 'extracts' available in the form of capsules are not recommended. Natural leaf powder of up to 5 teaspoons per day or fresh leaves can be taken by incorporating in any food preparations.

For moringa recipes, please refer to pages 137, 177.

GOND

(Gum Ghatti/Indian Edible Gum/ Gum Dhawda/ Gum Dawa)

Powerful anti-oxidant

Gum Ghatti is the amorphous translucent exudate of the tree *Anogeissus latifolia* (Family: Combretaceae) commonly known as axlewood tree. This deciduous tree is commonly found in the forests of the sub-Himalayan region, south India, Nepal, Myanmar, Srilanka and the Siwalik Hills.

The tree bark has been traditionally used in treating sores, boils, itch, snake and scorpion bites, leprosy and dysentery. The diuretic, wound-healing, hepatoprotective, anti-microbial, anti-ulcer and antioxidant properties of the bark have been proved in several studies. The bark is reported to contain phenolic compounds like gallic acid, ellagic acid, chebulic acid and flavonoids like rutin and quercetin which are powerful antioxidants.

Gum ghatti, the tree's exudate, is a calcium-magnesium salt composed of L-arabinose, D-galactose, D-mannose, D-xylose, and D-glucuronic acid and less than 1% of 6-deoxyhexose; a complex, non-starch polysaccharide. Basically, it is a mixture of complex sugars with a small protein content. It is used widely in food, pharmaceutical, paper and other industries mainly due to its excellent emulsification and thickening property. It is considered a tonic for women when given after childbirth. It has also proven to be a good stabilizer for ice-creams.

It has a regulatory status in the USA of "Generally considered as safe" or GRAS since 1976. Its acceptance in food in Japan, Latin America and other countries have made it an alternative hydrocolloid in the food industry.

Gum ghatti is easily confused with Tragacanth gum and Acacia gum which should be avoided. The reason for including gum ghatti as part of the special diet for the lactating mother is probably due to its complex sugars which can supply the required energy to the mother.

They also contain ellagic acid and glycosides of ellagic and flavellagic acid which are powerful antioxidants. Ellagic acid and its derivatives reduce the oxidative stress considerably. It is considered to be a powerful anti-cancer molecule.

A study has proved that treatment with gum ghatti at 750mg/kg produced a significant decrease in the serum cholesterol, triglyceride and elevation in HDL.

Intake limit: The World Health Organization committee on food additives have recently concluded that gum ghatti is unlikely to be a health concern and established an acceptable daily intake quantity as 'not specified'.

For recipes using gum ghatti, see pages 53, 65, 91, 95, 97, 105, 109, 125.

TURKEY BERRY

(Sundakkai, Thai brinjal)

The nutrition powerhouse

Turkey Berry *(Solanum torvum)* is a widely used herb in Indian and Chinese traditional medicine. It is a highly pharmacologically active member of the potato family. It is widely seen in Pakistan, India, Malaya, China, Philippines, and tropical America. Its edible fruits are used as a vegetable (an essential ingredient in Thai cuisine called Thai brinjal) and also added in dishes after sun-drying them, especially in Tamil Nadu. The fruits are considered to have antihypertensive, cardiovascular, anti-platelet aggregation, anti-microbial, antiviral (herpes), digestive and antioxidant effects. Its fruits are used to prepare haemopoetic tonics.

Solanum torvum contains a number of steroidal glycosides namely Torvosides A to L, non-alkaloidal constituents like sitosterol, stigmasterol, campesterol, apart from flavonoids, triterpenes, B and C vitamins and high concentration of iron.

The fruits are reported to strengthen the mucosal layer of the stomach by producing more mucus and bicarbonates thus neutralizing the increased gastric activity. The fruit decoctions are used to treat cough ailments and also liver and spleen enlargement.

A research study has shown a dose-dependent increase in the number of red blood cells and haemoglobin concentration with *Solanum torvum* extract. It has the capacity to reverse anaemia. *Solanum torvum* also contains vitamin C which may help in the reduction of iron in the ferric state to the ferrous state, resulting in the rapid absorption of iron, thus increasing the haemoglobin. It is reported that in most of the traditional homes in Ghana, it is customary to give diets containing *torvum* fruits with the intention of enhancing vitality and reversing the condition of anaemia.

A study was conducted to justify the use of a polyherbal formulation used traditionally for recuperation, rejuvenation and during pregnancy, lactation and convalescence in Ghana called 'Abemudro'. *Solanum torvum* is a part of the formulation and was found to contain the highest amount of most of the minerals analyzed, namely iron, magnesium, zinc, sodium and potassium.

Turkey berry was also found to contain around 11% of protein and a small percentage of vitamin B12, apart from vitamin B6 and vitamin C, all very important for maintaining a healthy blood profile.

As pregnant and lactating women are among the most nutritionally vulnerable groups, if a simple fruit containing most of the minerals and vitamins is useful for women post delivery, it should be given the attention it deserves.

Intake limit: There is no prescribed limit but 100gm of Turkey berries will meet the daily nutrient requirement of a healthy person including 18mg of iron. Pregnant women will require additional iron sources.

For recipes using Turkey berries (*Solanum torvum*) please refer to pages 43, 155.

India is a very diverse country. Its diversity extends to its cuisines too. Every region has its own food practices based on culture, availability of local ingredients, food preferences, climactic conditions and religious beliefs. There are a lot of foreign influences on the food too, like the Portuguese influence in Goan cuisine, Mughal and Persian influence in north Indian cuisines, etc. Over the years, the regional communities have absorbed these changes and at the same time steadfastly created their own practices.

Pregnancy and lactation are the periods during which the grandmother is most sought after in many Indian households. A woman is more likely to try traditional foods during this period if she believes that "if it worked for my grandmother and my mother, then it is good for me too". From home remedies to counter indigestion during pregnancy to special ladoos to increase lactation, every problem has a solution, only that the solution slightly varies with the states in India.

What follows is a compilation of recipes from different selected parts of India, namely Tamil Nadu, Kerala, Karnataka, Maharashtra, Rajasthan, Gujarat, Punjab and Himachal, Uttar Pradesh, West Bengal, Orissa and the Northeast.

The recipes contain some exquisite ingredients. Some of them are very unique to India and have roots in the practice of Ayurveda, one of the oldest medical practices in the world. Most of the ingredients are rich in flavonoids, polyphenols, and therefore, very active as antioxidants.

A column denoting the uses of the ingredient has also been included to benefit the reader. However, the uses are not limited to those specified. A calorie quotient with serving size is included with an author note on the recipe to guide the reader.

TRADITIONAL REGIONAL RECIPES OF INDIA

About the Traditional Recipes of India

- The recipes in the Traditional Indian Recipes section themselves are representatives of the tradition of each region of India. Some of them with multiple ingredients, like legiyam of Tamil Nadu or the Rajasthani battisa kada or the dashamoola kada address all the possible complaints a new mother can have.

- Many recipes include carminative and digestive elements like carom seeds, cumin seeds, fennel seeds since digestion-related issues are rampant during pregnancy. These ingredients are also included in the post-pregnancy period because the digestive health of the mother is important to spare the suckling newborn from colic issues.

- Many recipes are unique to the Indian subcontinent due to their ingredients—the banana flowers recipe from Bengal or the coconut flower preparation from Kerala.

- Areca nut ladoo is an inventive dish which surprises with its benefit of helping the newly delivered mom's uterus to regain its shape.

Icons used in this section:

For pregnancy

For lactation

Serving size

Calories per serving

- Several unique ladoos are made, namely the gond laddoo with edible gum, halim ladoo with gardencress seeds, muri ladoo with puffed rice, khus khus ladoo with poppy seeds, haldi ladoo with turmeric and methi ladoo with fenugreek seeds. The edible gum ladoo is a delightfully tasty yet inventive preparation loaded with goodness. The suthora or the foxnut and dry fruit and nut ladoo is an interesting and tasty combination.

- Many of the postnatal period recipes are rich in lactation aides, for instance the garlic halwa, sabudhana kheer and sooji kanji, which are all made with a few ingredients but designed for replenishing the reserves of the new mother.

- One of the hallmarks of the Indian cuisine, namely the 'chutney', is a regular in the pregnancy and lactation diets too. Chutney powders that burst with flavour are multipurpose, like the raw mango chutney of Kerala. They can be added to other dishes to add flavour or can be mixed as it is with rice and ghee. Recipes like the angaya podi that use the sun-dried Turkey berries and sesame-garlic chutney are regularly consumed by pregnant and lactating mothers. While Turkey berries are a rich source of iron, garlic and sesame with their galactagogue and calcium-rich properties are valuable additions to the diet.

- Healthy greens are a definite part of the pregnant and lactating mother's diet. The amaranth curry, dill leaves preparations and Malabar spinach recipe called 'vaali ambat' are regulars in the regional menus for these women.

- Fish-based dishes are preferred among non-vegetarian population compared to meat during this time. Sura puttu from Tamil Nadu made with shark fish is one such dish that is a sure-shot item in the lactating women's menu. Bengalis and northeastern states of India too include a lot of rui fish during this period.

- What can be observed from these recipes is that though the regional practices and preparations are diverse, there is a subtle pattern that unites them all. Every recipe serves a particular purpose and also comes with instructions for when to consume and for how long. These recipes use easily available ingredients and employ minimum skill for preparation. Majority of them are loaded with antioxidants and flavonoids as well as calories, especially if it is to be given to a lactating mother.

Calorie Quotient:

Low: Upto 200kcal per serving
Medium: 200kcal-400kcal per serving
High: Above 400kcal per serving

Madhavi was shuffling between impatience and excitement. She could not wait till 9 pm that night. Her mom, Lakshmi, was arriving from Chennai to help her with her delivery. Her husband Ravi had gone to Newark airport to receive her. Her mom was bringing with her a bag full of goodies from Mylapore. Lakshmi had made her customary trip to the famous Dabba Chetty Stores on Kutchery Road to collect the myriad herbs for the post-delivery 'legiyam'. She also had meticulously noted down the recipe from her mother who had delivered nine children herself. Lakshmi's mother used to make all preparations herself before she went into labour. Madhavi has heard her mom narrating this several times and so requested her mom to make it for her too. The legiyam has a halwa-like consistency and the new mother is supposed to have 1 teaspoon of the tasty preparation first thing in the morning and continue the practice for another three-four months.

One thing that makes Madhavi feel close to her Chennai home when living in suburban New York is her meal of angaaya podi mixed with ghee rice. Her favourite since childhood is also a preferred food item for pregnant and lactating mothers. It goes without saying that her mom brought refills of the podi. Madhavi had it all through her pregnancy to boost her iron and folic acid levels. For those who have not tasted angaaya podi, it would be intriguing to know that some people are almost addicted to it, since it is a dull black powder, not at all exciting in appearance! But it is packed with nutrients and flavour.

A queer sweet dish given to a lactating mother in Tamil Nadu is the poondu halwa or garlic halwa. It is supposed to help the mammary glands overflow! It is a delightfully tasty dish but laborious to make since the garlic pods have to be peeled patiently. Lakshmi later reminisced fondly how her younger sisters used to line up to taste it when it was made for her when Madhavi was born.

If you ask Madhavi or for that matter any Tamilian to name their comfort food, the majority will vote for rasam! It is a watery lentil preparation bursting with flavour and goodness. One of the staple items in the everyday menu, it can be prepared with some variations like adding kandathippili and arisithippili to give it some additional medicinal properties. Amaranth greens are also widely used during pregnancy and even after delivery.

TAMIL NADU

Legiyam Podi (Post-childbirth Herb Powder)

Ingredients

 1tsp  20kcal

English	Tamil	Amount	Use
Dry ginger	*Sukku*	50gm	Helps in blood circulation
Lesser galangal	*Chithrathai*	50gm	Reduces cramps
Long pepper fruit	*Arisithippili*	50gm	Helps uterus to return to normal size
Long pepper root	*Kandathippili*	50gm	Anti-oxidant, aids digestion
Liquorice	*Adhi maduram*	50gm	Harmoniser and pacifier
False black pepper	*Vayuvilangam*	50gm	For healthy skin and anti-fungal
Wild or spiral ginger	*Koshtam*	50gm	Helps to beat allergens and skin itching
Cinnamon	*Lavangapattai*	4 pieces of 1"	Reduces inflammatory mediators in the body
Himalayan silver fir	*Taalisapatri*	10gm	Disgorges mucus from windpipe.
Cardamom seeds	*Ela arisi*	5-10gm	Antacid
Dill seeds	*Sadakuppai*	5-10gm	Prevents colic in feeding infant
Black pepper	*Milagu*	50gm	Metabolic booster and anti-inflammatory
Chinese liquorice	*Parangipattai*	3"	Rich in flavonoids
Indian atees	*Adhividayam*	2tsp	Analgesic
Poppy seeds	*Khasa Khasa*	25gm	High in Calcium
Cumin seeds	*Jeeragam*	50gm	Aids digestion
Cloves	*Kraambu*	25 nos	Reduces stomach inflammation
Coriander seeds	*Kothamalli virai*	1 cup	Aids digestion
Nutmeg	*Jaadikkai*	1 piece	Soothes nerves, reduces tension and anxiety
Tailed pepper/ Java pepper/ Cubeb	*Vaalmilagu*	10gm	Aids digestion, helps clear mucus from airways
Mace	*Jaadipathiri*	10gm	Alleviates depression, releases serotonin
Indian ginseng/ Ashwagandha	*Amukkara kizhangu*	50gm	Decreases stress, improves quality of reproductive tissues
Harad	*Kadukkai*	4 nos	Regulates blood levels, relieves constipation, aids weight loss
Ajwain/ Carrom seeds	*Omam*	400gm	Aids digestion, beats flatulence

(Cont...)

Poondu Halwa (Garlic Halwa)

(...cont) Legiyam Podi

Method

Clean all the herbs and dry roast separately. Grind to a powder and store in an airtight container.

Make small batches of the legiyam as follows:

1. Make a thick syrup by heating 25gm of palm sugar with water.
2. Add 4 tablespoons of the legiyam powder and cook till it becomes a thick paste.
3. Add a tablespoon of ghee.

Makes 4 tablespoons of legiyam. Take 1 teaspoon of legiyam first thing in the morning.

Poondu Halwa (Garlic Halwa)

Ingredients

 ½ cup 

133kcal

English	Tamil	Amount	Use
Cow's milk	*Pasum paal*	500ml	Rich source of protein, calcium and vitamins
Garlic pods	*Poondu*	50gm	Antifungal, helps maintain milk supply in breasts and helps avoid mastitis in breastfeeding moms
Palm sugar	*Pana vellam*	As per sweetness	Low glycemic index, rich in vitamins, minerals, antioxidants and flavonoids. Rich in inositol needed for healthy cell formation
Ghee	*Nei*	1tsp	Good source of fat
Saffron	*Kunkumapoo*	Few strands	Boosts haemoglobin and is a mood stabilizer

Method

1. Cook the cleaned garlic pods in milk till it thickens.
2. Mash it well and add palm sugar.
3. Remove from heat and add ghee and strands of saffron.

Makes 2 cups. Have half cup at bedtime.

Angaya Podi (Dry Chutney Powder)

Ingredients

 2tsp  20kcal

English	Tamil	Amount	Use
Sun-dried Turkey berry	Sundakkai vathal	2tbsp	Very rich source of vitamin A, vitamin C and iron
Sun-dried black night shade fruit/sunberry/ wonder berry	*Manathakkali vathal*	2tbsp	Heals ulcers, rich in B-Complex vitamins
Dried neem flowers	*Veppam poo*	2tbsp	Improves digestive health, reduces bile, removes intestinal worms
Dried ginger powder	*Sukku podi*	1tsp	Helps in blood circulation, aids to relieve headache and migraine
Split Bengal gram	*Kadalai paruppu*	1tbsp	Source of protein and fibre
Split black gram (white)	*Ulundu*	2tbsp	Source of protein and fibre
Split red gram	*Thuvaram paruppu*	2tbsp	Source of protein and fibre
Red chillies	*Milagai vatral*	4	Rich in flavonoids
Black pepper	*Milagu*	1tbsp	Metabolic booster and anti-inflammatory
Cumin seeds	*Jeeragam*	1tbsp	Aids digestion
Asafoetida	*Perungayam*	1tsp	Carminative, antiviral, antioxidant

Method

1. Dry roast Turkey berry, sunberry and neem flowers in a wok till it becomes dark in colour.
2. Separately dry roast the other ingredients one by one.
3. Add required salt, and powder everything together.

Makes 1.5 cups of podi; 2 teaspoon powder to be mixed with hot ghee rice.

Suraa Puttu (Scrambled White Shark Fish)

Ingredients

 1 cup  154kcal

English	Tamil	Amount	Use
White shark fish	*Paal suraa*	250gm	Rich source of protein, helps in milk production. Good source of omega 3 fatty acids
Shallots	*Chinna vengayaam*	6 nos.	Rich source of potassium, increases production of antioxidant glutathione
Fennel seeds	*Sombu*	½tsp	Anti-flatulent
Oil, salt, turmeric and pepper	*Ennai, uppu, manjal and milagu*	As required	

Method

1. Cut the shark fish into pieces and apply some salt and turmeric powder.
2. Cook it in hot boiling water and peel off the skin.
3. Scramble the boiled fish.
4. Fry fennel seeds and shallots in oil. Add the scrambled fish to it and sauté.
5. Add salt and pepper powder as required.

Makes 2 cups. 1 cup of preparation daily boosts the protein intake by 25gm.

Kandathippili Rasam (Long Pepper Soup)

Ingredients

 1 cup  38kcal

English	Tamil	Amount	Use
Long pepper root	*Kandathippili*	4 nos of 1"	Anti-oxidant, aids digestion
Long pepper fruit	*Arisithippili*	2 pieces	Helps uterus to return to normal size
Cumin seeds	*Jeeragam*	½tsp	Aids digestion
Coriander seeds	*Kothamalli virai*	2tsp	Aids digestion
Black pepper	*Milagu*	1.5tsp	Metabolic booster and anti-inflammatory
Split red gram	*Thuvaram paruppu*	2tsp	Good vegetarian protein source

Method

Dry roast each ingredient separately and make a fine powder. You can store this dry roasted powder to use at a later time as well.

Ingredients for the rasam:

- One lime-sized ball of tamarind
- 2 cups of water
- Salt to taste

1. Add a cup of boiling water to the tamarind and let it soak for 15 minutes. Squeeze out and extract the tamarind water and remove the seeds/fibre if any.
2. Boil this extracted tamarind by adding another cup of water with salt. (As per need, you could add some more water). After it continues boiling for 3 minutes, add the above powder to it and let it boil a bit more and turn off the heat.

Ingredients for tempering:

- 1 teaspoon ghee
- ½ teaspoon mustard seeds
- A few curry leaves

1. Take a small saucepan and add a teaspoon of ghee. Add mustard seeds. Let it splutter.
2. Add curry leaves and turn off the heat. Add this into the rasam.

Makes 2 cups. Can have up to 2 standard cups per day.

Sirukkerai Masiyal (Tropical Amaranth Curry)

Ingredients

 1 cup 

70kcal

English	Tamil	Amount	Use
Tropical amaranth greens *(Amaranthus polygonoides)*	*Sirukkeerai*	1 bunch	High in iron and folic acid
Split green gram dal	*Payatham paruppu*	1tbsp	Good protein source
Shallots	*Chinna vengayam*	8 finely chopped	Rich source of potassium, increases production of master antioxidant - glutathione
Garlic	*Poondu*	2 crushed	Antifungal, helps maintain milk supply in breasts and helps avoid mastitis in breastfeeding moms
Mustard seeds	*Kadugu*	¼tsp	Rich in calcium, vitamin A and E
Cumin seeds	*Jeeragam*	¼tsp	Aids digestion
Asafoetida	*Perungaayam*	A pinch	Anti-flatulent
Turmeric powder	*Manjal*	A pinch	Anti-microbial
Dry red chilli	*Milagai vatral*	2 nos.	Rich in flavonoids
Salt	*Uppu*	As per taste	
Oil	*Ennai*	2tsp	

Method

1. Pluck the amaranth leaves and tender stems from the bunch, wash them well and strain the water.
2. Wash the green gram dal and cook in 2 cups of water with a pinch of turmeric.
3. While the dal is cooking, in a small pan heat oil, add mustard, and let it splutter, add dry red chillies, cumin and asafoetida.
4. After a few seconds, add crushed garlic and finely chopped small onions and sauté till it turns translucent.
5. Once the dal is cooked, add the greens and cook together for 5 minutes adding little water if required. Mash it up slightly with a hand blender.
6. Add the mustard tempering and the sautéed onion, garlic to the greens and dal mixture.
7. Add salt to taste and mix.

Makes 2 cups. Can have 1 to 2 cups per day.

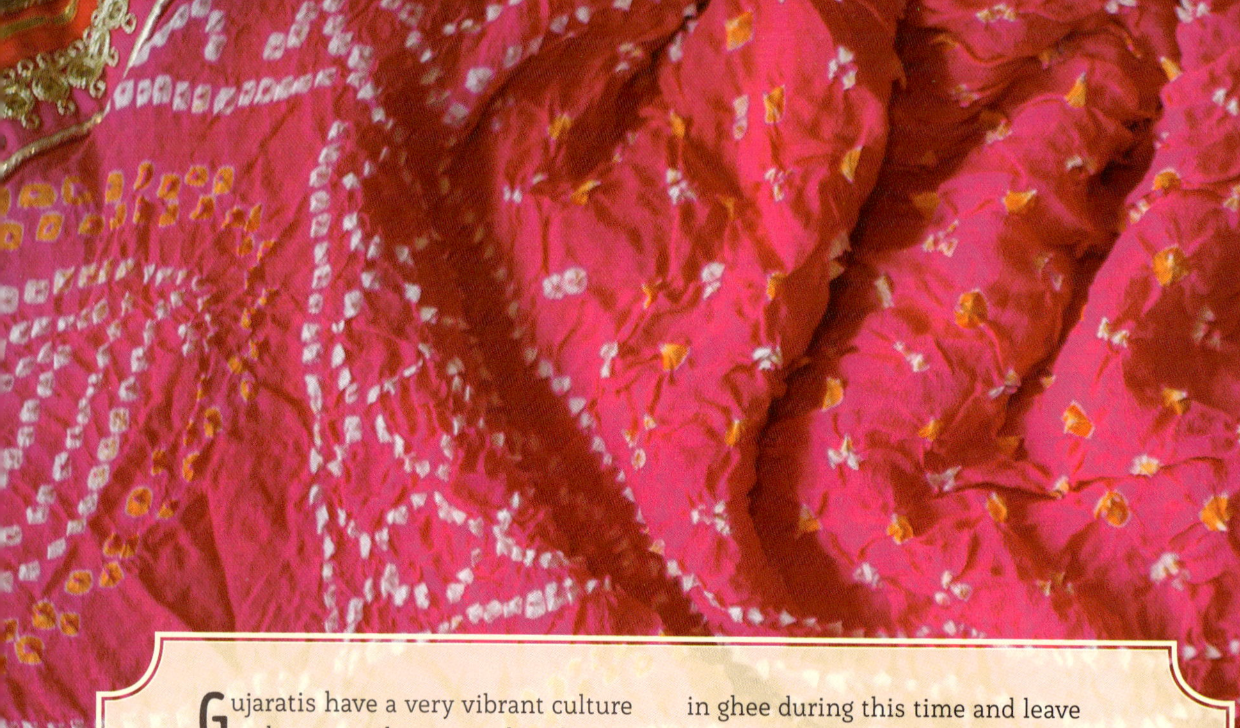

Gujaratis have a very vibrant culture and are very deep-rooted in their beliefs whether they be Jains or Kucchis or any other subsection. They are a community with a very evident proverbial sweettooth. This is reflected in their post-pregnancy diet where sugar, jaggery and coconut are common features in all the recipes.

When Darshana got pregnant, little did she realize that she would be subjected to an avalanche of information, courtesy her mother, aunts, friends, colleagues and doctors. Each one of them had a different take on what to eat or not to eat, and it was very confusing for her. She decided to find out for herself the most effective practices.

She was surprised to know that in Gujarati households the preparation for postpartum care starts right from the seventh month of pregnancy. They soak natural edible gum locally called 'gond' in ghee during this time and leave it for three months. Post a normal delivery, if it is winter, they make an interesting drink called 'Raab'. A specially spiced water, mouth freshener and tea-like concoction are all prepared for the new mother to increase digestion.

Darshana's mom-in-law gave her a packet of ganthoda powder she bought in the market that day. Darshana had no idea about it. After researching, she found out that a concoction of ganthoda powder (made from the root of long pepper), water, dry ginger and jaggery is a natural remedy for gastric discomfort. It is also a rich source of magnesium.

Several types of calorie- and nutrient-rich halwas and ladoos are included in the diet to aid lactation. Her aunt told her about the herb 'shatavari', which is consumed at night and raw garlic is consumed early morning to improve breast milk production.

GUJARAT

Top: Raab (Drink)

Raab (Drink)

Ingredients

 1 cup  215kcal

English	Gujarati	Amount	Use
Natural edible gum	*Gundar*	2tsp	High fibre and complex carbohydrate
Dry ginger powder	*Sunth*	1tsp	Anti-inflammatory
Jaggery	*Gol*	To taste	Rich in iron
Ghee	*Ghee*	1tbsp	Source of conjugated linoleic acid and fat soluble vitamins

Method

1. The edible gum is sautéed in ghee.
2. Then dry ginger, jaggery and water is added.
3. If it is summer, then dry ginger is not added in the raab and sometimes jaggery is substituted by sugar.

Makes 1 cup. Can have 1 cup per day, taking small sips over time.

Ghaun No Sheero (Wheat Flour Halwa)

Ingredients

 ½ cup  360kcal

English	Gujarati	Amount	Use
Wheat flour	*Ghaun no lot*	50gm	Dietary fibre, and good carbohydrate and micronutrient source
Jaggery	*Gol*	50gm	Rich in iron
Ghee	*Ghee*	30gm	Source of conjugated linoleic acid (CLA) and fat-soluble vitamins
Garden cress seeds	*Asariyo*	5gm	Rich in iron
Almonds	*Badam*	15gm	Rich in protein and vitamin E
Water	*Paani*	200ml	

Method

1. Boil the water with jaggery and keep aside.
2. Sauté the almonds, seeds and flour in ghee till golden brown.
3. Then add the boiled water and make the halwa of flowy consistency. Add more water if required.

Makes 1 cup. Half cup can be consumed as a breakfast item.

Methi Ane Khus Na Laadu (Fenugreek and Poppy Seed Ladoo) 

Ingredients

English	Gujarati	Amount	Use
Fenugreek seeds	*Methi*	50gm	Galactagogue
Poppy seeds	*Khaskhas*	15gm	Rich calcium source, immunity booster
Dry coconut	*Sukku kopru*	200gm	Strengthens connective tissue
Dates	*Kharek*	50gm	Vitamin A,C,E & Mg
Jaggery	*Gor*	100gm	Natural cleansing agent
Natural edible gum	*Gundar*	25gm	Reduces oxidative stress and provides energy
Almonds	*Badam*	25gm	Protein, magnesium and vitamin E

Method

1. Roast fenugreek seeds and powder them.
2. Fry the edible gum and powder it.
3. Grate the jaggery, chop the almonds and keep aside.
4. Roast dry coconut on low flame.
5. Combine all the other ingredients and mix with the grated jaggery to make ladoos.

Makes 20 lemon-sized ladoos. One ladoo a day can be taken as a snack. Sweetness can be reduced if required.

Digestive Munch

Ingredients

 1tsp  20kcal

English	Gujarati	Amount	Use
Cumin seeds	*Jeera*	1tsp	Contains thymol which increases breast milk
Raisins	*Draksh*	5 pcs.	Rich in iron
Fennel seeds	*Variyali*	1tsp	Balances stomach acids

Method

1. Soak all the ingredients overnight.
2. Grind in the morning and serve as a digestive munch.

Can have up to 3 teaspoons per day.

Mouth Freshener

Ingredients

 1tsp  25kcal

English	Gujarati	Amount	Use
Dill Seeds	*Suva*	50gm	Digestive, galactagogue
Dry coconut	*Sukku kopru*	50gm	Reduces cellulite
Sesame seeds	*Til*	50gm	Increasing breast milk
Fennel seeds	*Variyari*	50gm	Anti-flatulent
Salt	*Meethu*	To taste	
Turmeric	*Haldar*	1 pinch	Antibacterial

Method

1. Lightly roast dill, sesame and fennel seeds.
2. Add rest of the ingredients and store.

Can have up to 3 teaspoons per day.

Special Tea

Ingredients

 1 cup  50kcal

English	Gujarati	Amount	Use
Dill seeds	*Suva*	2tsp	Digestive, galactagogue
Jaggery	*Gol*	To taste	Removes blood impurity
Ghee	*Ghee*	1tsp	Rich in fat soluble vitamins
Water	*Paani*	250ml	

Method

1. The seeds are soaked overnight and then boiled in water.
2. Then ghee and jaggery is added to the tea.
3. This concoction is given after 4 to 5 days of delivery.

Author's Note: *Can have 1 cup per day.*

Flavored Drinking Water

Ingredients

 1 cup  None

English	Gujarati	Amount	Use
Dry ginger powder	*Sunth*	A pinch	Digestive
Water	*Paani*	1 litre	

Method

1. Boiled water is prepared by adding a pinch of dry ginger powder for drinking sip by sip throughout the day.

Author's Note: *Can consume up to 1 litre per day.*

Bajra No Sheero (Pearl Millet Halwa)

Ingredients

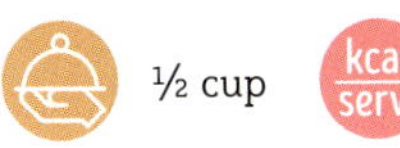 ½ cup 

310kcal

English	Gujarati	Amount	Use
Pearl millet	*Bajra no lot*	50gm	Rich in folic acid and iron
Jaggery powder	*Gol*	50gm	Rich in iron and minerals
Ghee	*Ghee*	30gm	Source of fat soluble vitamins and CLA
Peppercorn (crushed)	*Mari*	1tsp	Improves digestion, carminative
Cardamom powder	*Elachi*	½tsp	Anti-inflammatory
Water	*Paani*	200ml	

Method

1. Sauté the flour in ghee.
2. Dissolve jaggery in the water by slightly warming.
3. Add the jaggery water to the flour and keep stirring till a halwa consistency is reached.
4. Add pepper and cardamom.

Makes 1 cup. Have half cup for breakfast or as a heavy snack.

Jaspreet, a Punjabi by birth, was brought up in the cool hills of Shimla. She had a taste for both the typical Punjabi food and the simple 'pahadi' food enriched with all the ingredients of the hills.

Settled in Canada, her connection to the practices of Himachal is her *bua* (aunt). She told Jaspreet that the initial pregnancy months are when cooling foods like seera are given. In the ninth month the emphasis is on building the mother's strength, so calorie-rich food with ghee and nuts are given. Special care of the lactating mother is also taken when dishes like khairani and moong halwa are prepared.

Punjabis frequently make paneer (homemade cottage cheese) dishes during the last trimester of pregnancy and during the lactation period.

Women are also given spiced water throughout the pregnancy to aid in digestion.

PUNJAB & HIMACHAL PRADESH

Khairani (Dry Fruits in Milk Base)

Khairani is a nutritious drink given to combat post-natal stress.

Ingredients

 1 cup 

356kcal

English	Punjabi	Amount	Use
Dry ginger powder	Sauth	½tsp	Helps in blood circulation, aids to relieve headache and migraine
Crushed almonds	*Badam*	1tbsp	High in magnesium
Cashew nuts	*Kanju*	1tbsp	High in oleic acid & good for heart
Dry coconut shreds	*Nariyal*	1tbsp	The high lauric acid contents give antibacterial, anti-inflammatory and antiviral properties
Dates	*Khajur*	4 pcs. deseeded	Vitamin A,C,E & Mg
Dried melon seeds	*Magaz beej*	1tsp	Rich in micronutrients
Milk	*Doodh*	450ml	Rich source of protein, calcium and vitamins
Sugar	*Chini*	2tsp	

Method

1. Roast dry ginger powder in ghee till it turns golden brown.
2. Add the nuts and seeds and roast for a minute.
3. Pour the milk and sugar and let it simmer till it reduces to half the quantity.
4. Add the dates as paste and serve hot.

Makes 2 cups. Serving size of one cup should be adhered to. Sugar can be avoided to reduce calories.

Moong Dal Halwa (Split Green Gram Halwa)

Ingredients

 ½ cup 

308kcal

English	Punjabi	Amount	Use
Split green gram	*Moong dal*	50gm	Macronutrients
Crushed almonds	*Badam*	1tbsp	High in magnesium
Dry coconut shreds	*Nariyal*	1tbsp	The high lauric acid contents give antibacterial, anti-inflammatory and antiviral properties
Dates	*Khajur*	1tbsp	Vitamin A,C,E & Mg
Raisins	*Kismis*	1tbsp	Rich in vitamin B-Complex, iron and potassium
Dry ginger powder	*Sauth*	½tsp	Helps in blood circulation, aids to relieve headache and migraine
Ghee	*Ghee*	25gm	Good source of fat
Sugar	*Chini*	50gm	
Natural edible gum	*Gond*	1tbsp	Antioxidant, controls lipid levels, complex carbohydrate

Method

1. Soak split green gram overnight and grind it into a paste.
2. Grind the rest of the ingredients, except raisins, dates, dry coconut shreds and sugar, and add to the paste.
3. Take ghee in a pan and sauté all the ingredients till it turns reddish brown.
4. Add powdered sugar and warm water to get the proper consistency of halwa. Then garnish with raisins and dates.

Makes 1.5 cups. Serving size should be adhered to because of high calories per serving. Sugar can be completely replaced with dates and raisins.

Seera (Germinated Wheat Fudge)

P L

This is a very healthy snack given to pregnant women in Himachal as it has cooling properties and is believed to prevent miscarriage. Seera is a nutritious, easily digestible traditional fermented food made from whole wheat grain. It is also called Nishasta. It is very rich in microflora, which is helpful for gut health.

Seera balls: Wheat grains are soaked in water for 2-3 days so as to allow fermentation to occur by natural microflora. After 2-3 days the grains are ground, steeping is done when the starch grains and some proteins settle down. Then the bran is separated. Starch and proteins are removed, sundried and this is called 'seera'. The dried material is made into slurry by soaking in water; which is then poured into hot ghee, with sugar, cooked and served as a sweet dish/snack.

Seera is considered to be nutritious and easily digestible and a quick snack. It is prepared for pregnant women or offered to the guests as a sweet dish in the rural/urban areas of Kullu, Kangra, Mandi and Chamba districts.

Ingredients

 ½ cup 

123kcal

English	Pahari	Amount	Use
Seera balls	*Seera*	50gm	Rich in microflora, good source of energy
Ghee	*Ghee*	20gm	
Sugar	*Chini*	40gm	

Method

1. Soak the seera balls in water till it softens.
2. Take ghee in a pan and sauté the seera in it, stirring continuously.
3. Add sugar and cook on slow flame till it leaves ghee.

Makes 2 cups. Can swap the sugar with dates, figs, raisins or jaggery.

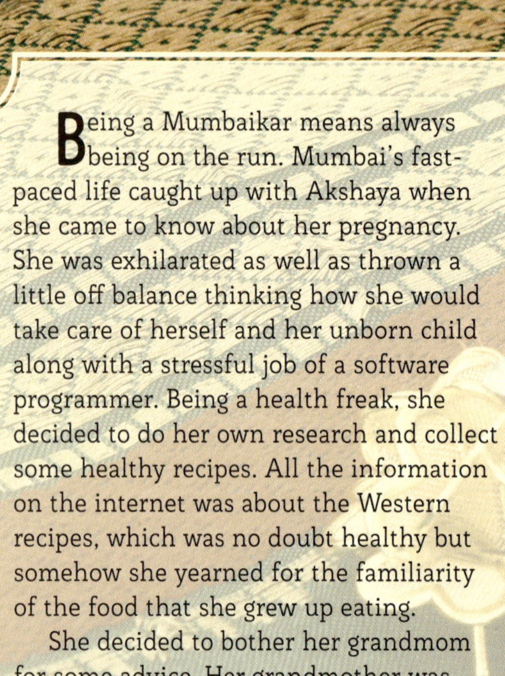

Being a Mumbaikar means always being on the run. Mumbai's fast-paced life caught up with Akshaya when she came to know about her pregnancy. She was exhilarated as well as thrown a little off balance thinking how she would take care of herself and her unborn child along with a stressful job of a software programmer. Being a health freak, she decided to do her own research and collect some healthy recipes. All the information on the internet was about the Western recipes, which was no doubt healthy but somehow she yearned for the familiarity of the food that she grew up eating.

She decided to bother her grandmom for some advice. Her grandmother was glad Akshaya asked about the traditional foods and passed on some treasured recipes. Akshaya also realized that it actually had all the essential nutrients and balance for a complete meal. For example, aliv laddoos that are specially made for lactating mothers have a high iron content. Methi laddoos are also recommended daily to aid lactation. Poppy seed kheer is rich in calcium. Slowly, the whole idea and collective wisdom behind these dishes dawned on Akshaya.

Fenugreek seed ladoos and edible gum ladoos also form an integral part of the Maharashtrian postpartum diet. For iron and calcium, chicken soup and lamb leg soup (non-spicy) is also given within the first 10-12 days of delivery, for at least 2-3 times a day. They also believe that soda fish is good for lactation. Maharashtrian mothers consume dry bombil fish for strength and immunity. Foods like bitter gourd, cluster beans, French beans are avoided during this period as it is believed to decrease lactation.

MAHARASHTRA

Methichi Kheer (Fenugreek Seed Pudding)

Methichi Kheer (Fenugreek Seed Pudding)

Ingredients

 1 cup  281kcal

English	Marathi	Amount	Use
Fenugreek seeds	*Methi*	¼ cup	Galactagogue
Rice	*Tandul*	⅓ cup	Macronutrients rich
Grated fresh coconut	*Khobra*	½ cup	Antibacterial, anti-inflammatory and antiviral
Jaggery	*Gul*	30gm	Rich in iron
Ghee	*Tup*	1tsp	Good fats
Cardamom powder	*Velchi*	½tsp	Digestive

Method

1. Pressure cook rice, fenugreek and coconut together with enough water.
2. After it is cooked add jaggery and cook on slow fire stirring continuously till it blends properly.
3. Add ghee and cardamom powder on top for flavour.

Makes 2 cups. 1 cup can be a filling snack.

Khaskhaschi Kheer (Poppy Seed Pudding)

Ingredients

 ½ cup  150kcal

English	Marathi	Amount	Use
Poppy seeds	*Khaskhas*	15gm	Rich calcium source, immunity booster
Cow's milk	*Dudh*	250ml	Rich source of protein, calcium and vitamins
Almonds	*Badam*	10 pcs.	Protein, magnesium and vitamin E
Sugar	*Sakhar*	30gm	Carbohydrate

Method

1. Soak the poppy seeds overnight.
2. Blend almonds and poppy seeds in a mixer and make a paste.
3. Bring the milk to a boil and add the paste and cook for sometime.
4. Then add sugar and serve hot.

Makes 1.5 cups. Can swap sugar with dry fruits.

Alivche Ladoo (Garden Cress Seed Ladoos)

Ingredients

1 ladoo 144kcal

English	Marathi	Amount	Use
Garden cress seeds	*Aliv*	50gm	Rich in iron
Nutmeg	*Jayphal*	½tsp	Soothes nerves, reduces tension and anxiety
Grated fresh coconut	*Khobra*	2tbsp	The high lauric acid contents give antibacterial, anti-inflammatory and antiviral properties
Cardamom	*Velchi*	5-6 pcs.	Antacid
Jaggery	*Gul*	2 cups (grated)	Rich in iron

Method

1. Wash the aliv seeds and dry it.
2. Then mix it with grated fresh coconut.
3. Keep aside in a cool place for 3 hours.
4. Add jaggery and allow it to simmer on slow heat till the mixture starts separating from the pan.
5. Add nutmeg and crushed cardamom and make ladoos.

Makes 10 lemon-sized ladoos weighing about 20-25gm each. Good iron booster. Store refrigerated.

Top: Khobra-Lahsunchi Chutney (Coconut-Garlic Chutney)
Bottom: Lahsun-Tilachi Chutney (Garlic-Sesame Chutney)

Khobra-Lahsunchi Chutney (Coconut-Garlic Chutney)  

 1tbsp  22kcal

Ingredients

English	Marathi	Amount	Use
Grated coconut	*Khobra*	1/2 cup	Anti-inflammatory and antiviral
Garlic	*Lehsun*	7 cloves	Antifungal, helps maintain milk supply in breasts and helps avoid mastitis in breastfeeding moms
Black pepper	*Kali miri*	10 no.	Metabolic booster and anti-inflammatory
Fennel seeds	*Badi shev*	½ cup	Anti-flatulent
Salt	*Meeth*	To taste	

Method

1. Roast all the items including salt.
2. Mix all the ingredients and grind it.

Author's Note

Makes 10 tablespoons.
Keep refrigerated

Lahsun-Tilachi Chutney (Garlic-Sesame Chutney)  

 1tbsp  80kcal

Ingredients

English	Marathi	Amount	Use
Sesame seeds	*Tila*	1 cup	Increasing breast milk, high in calcium
Garlic	*Lehsun*	8 cloves	Antifungal, helps maintain milk supply in breasts and helps avoid mastitis in breastfeeding moms
Green chilli	*Mirchi*	1 no.	Rich in flavonoids
Salt	*Meeth*	To taste	

Method

3. Roast sesame seeds.
4. Add the rest of the ingredients and pound to make a dry chutney.

Author's Note

Makes 10 tablespoons.

Ananya is a happy-go-lucky Manglorean living in the coastal region of Goa. She works in tourism sector but when it comes to food nothing foreign allures her. She has always been a seafood lover. Having had a foreign education and staying away from parents meant that she could not learn exactly how to prepare her community's cuisine though she enjoyed eating it. So, when she got pregnant and got to stay at her mother's house for prolonged duration, she made it a point to learn about the traditional diet given to women post-delivery among her community.

She found out that the diet consists mostly of fishes and vegetables. Sardines and mackerel are predominantly consumed. In vegetables, elephant yam (suran) with garlic is consumed widely probably because of its high iron content. Coconut oil is the cooking medium used. In lentils, only split pigeon peas (tuvar) with red rice is given. A soup made from banana flower is given for lactation.

Different types of porridge called 'kanji' is very famous in Karnataka.

KARNATAKA

Top: Jeera Neeru (Black Cumin Tea)
Bottom: Ragi Kanji (Finger Millet Porridge)

Jeera Neeru (Black Cumin Tea)

Ingredients

English	Kannada	Amount	Use
Black cumin	*Kari jeerige*	1tsp	Enhances immunity
Black pepper	*Kari menasu*	1 pinch	Metabolic booster and anti-inflammatory
Jaggery	*Bella*	To taste	Rich in iron
Water	*Neeru*	200ml	

Method

1. Brew all the ingredients except jaggery for some time.
2. Add jaggery and after 2 minutes strain and drink like a tea.

Makes 1 cup of jeera neeru.

Ragi Kanji (Finger Millet Porridge)

Ingredients

1 cup made with 1 tablespoon powder

110kcal with milk

English	Kannada	Amount	Use
Finger millet	*Ragi*	250gm	Rich in calcium
Wheat	*Godhi*	200gm	Macro nutrients
Red rice	*Kempu akki*	½ cup	Macro nutrients
Roasted Bengal gram	*Huri kadale*	½ cup	High in protein
Almonds, cashews	*Badami, godambi*	1 cup	High in magnesium
Cardamom	*Elakki*	1tsp	Antacid

Method

1. Soak ragi overnight. Next day spread it on a wet cloth and leave it to sprout.
2. Dry roast sprouted ragi, wheat, rice and gram separately till a red tinge appears.
3. Grind into a fine powder.
4. Add the nuts powder and cardamom powder, mix well and store.
5. Make a slurry of 1 to 2 tablespoons of kanji powder in water and cook till it forms a uniform paste.
6. Add some milk and sweetening before serving.

Makes 3 cups of kanji powder. Can consume up to 2 cups of kanji a day. Limit the sweetening.

Top: Sooji Kanji (Semolina Porridge)
Bottom: Sunthi Kanji (Dry Ginger Porridge)

Sooji Kanji (Semolina Porridge)

Ingredients

 1 cup  145kcal

English	Kannada	Amount	Use
Semolina	*Ravae*	2tbsp	Macronutrients
Black pepper	*Kari menasu*	1 pinch	Metabolic booster and anti-inflammatory
Ghee	*Tuppa*	1tsp	Good source of fat
Salt	*Uppu*	To taste	

Method

1. Take a pan and roast the semolina in the ghee.
2. When red, add salt and black pepper and water to make it of a very loose consistency.

Makes 1 cup.

Sunthi Kanji (Dry Ginger Porridge)

Ingredients

 1 cup  45kcal

English	Kannada	Amount	Use
Dry ginger	*Saunth*	1 pinch	Helps in blood circulation
Black pepper	*Kari menasu*	1 pinch	Metabolic booster and anti-inflammatory
Ghee	*Tuppa*	1tsp	Good source of fat
Black cumin	*Kari jeerige*	½tsp	Enhances immunity
Water	*Neeru*	200ml	

Method

1. Take a pan and roast the black cumin in the ghee till it becomes dark brown.
2. Add water, dry ginger, pepper powder and boil together for 5 minutes.

Makes 1 cup.

Vaali Ambat (Malabar Spinach Curry)

This is consumed regularly during pregnancy.

Ingredients

 1 cup  188kcal

English	Kannada	Amount	Use
Split pigeon peas	*Thogari bele*	¼ cup	Good source of protein
Malabar spinach	*Vaali bhaji*	1 bunch	High in iron
Onion	*Trulli*	1 small	Prebiotic
Garlic	*Irulli*	4 big cloves	High allicin content
Fresh grated coconut	*Thenginakaayi thuri*	½ cup	The high lauric acid contents give antibacterial, anti-inflammatory and antiviral properties
Dry red chillies	*Kempu menasinakai*	5 pcs.	Rich in flavanoids
Coriander seeds	*Kottambari*	1tbsp	Relieves menstrual disorder
Tamarind	*Hunisehannu*	½tsp	Vitamin B3
Turmeric	*Harshina*	¼tsp	Anti-inflammatory
Salt	*Uppu*	To taste	
Oil	*Taila*	1tsp	

Method

1. Pressure cook the split pigeon peas in one cup water.
2. Take few drops of oil in a pan and roast coriander seeds and dry chilies till slightly dark, and chilies turn crisp.
3. Grind grated coconut, turmeric, tamarind, roasted chilies, and coriander seeds to a slightly coarse paste.
4. In a big pot, add cooked dal, chopped Malabar spinach and onions.
5. Mix and cook it covered. Add water if required.
6. Add the coconut paste and salt to the pot when veggies are about half cooked. Cook it covered till the stems are cooked and the desired consistency is obtained.
7. Sauté the crushed garlic in the oil and temper the dish.

Makes 2 cups. This dish is a good iron booster.

Sabsige Soppu Bhaat (Dill Leaves Rice)

Dill leaves, because of their nutritive qualities, are used in both rice and rasam prepared for the nursing mother.

Ingredients

 1 cup 

231kcal

English	Kannada	Amount	Use
Basmati rice	*Akki*	1 cup	Macronutrients
Dill leaves	*Sabsige elegalu*	¾ bunch	Prevents colic in feeding infant
Mixed vegetables	*Tarkarigalu*	½ cup	Vitamins & minerals
Ghee	*Tuppa*	1tsp	Good source of fat
Turmeric	*Harshina*	½tsp	Anti-inflammatory
Lemon juice	*Nimbe rasaa*	1tsp	Immunity booster
Dry masala			
Cumin	*Jirige*	1tsp	Thymol increases breast milk
Coriander seeds	*Kottambari beeja*	1tsp	Digestive, high in calcium
Fennel seeds	*Sompu*	1tsp	Anti-flatulent
Cinnamon	*Dalcinni*	2" stick	Antioxidant, reduces insulin resistance
Cardamoms	*Elakki*	1-2	Antacid
Cloves	*Lavanga*	5-7	Dental health & digestion
Bay leaf	*Lavangada ele*	1-2	Anti-flatulent
Black peppercorn	*Kari menasu*	10-12	Metabolic booster and anti-inflammatory

Method

1. Powder all the ingredients for the dry masala in a blender and keep aside. Make sure not to add any water while powdering.
2. Heat ghee in a heavy bottomed pan and temper cumin seeds.
3. Add soaked rice (after draining the water) to the pan and sauté for minute or two.
4. Add the dry masala powder, mixed vegetables and the chopped dill leaves.
5. Pour about 1.5 cups of water, salt and mix well. Bring to boil and then cook covered on medium heat for about 10 minutes or until done.
6. Add lemon juice after switching off the fire.

Makes 3 cups. A good substitute for plain rice.

Sabsige Soppu Saaru (Dill Leaves Soup)

Ingredients

 1 cup  39kcal

English	Kannada	Amount	Use
Dill leaves	*Sabsige elegalu*	½ cup chopped	Prevents colic in feeding infant
Cumin	*Jirige*	¼tsp	Thymol content increases the breast milk
Coriander seeds	*Kothambari beeja*	1tsp	Relieves menstrual disorders, rich in calcium
Black pepper	*Kari menasu*	¼ to ½tsp	Metabolic booster and anti-inflammatory
Fresh grated coconut	*Tenginakayi thuri*	¼ cup	The high lauric acid contents give antibacterial, anti-inflammatory and antiviral properties
Green chillies	*Hasi menasinaka*	1	Rich in flavonoids
Tamarind	*Hunasehannu*	To taste	Vitamin B3
Jaggery	*Bella*	Optional	Rich in iron
Salt	*Uppu*	To taste	
Mustard seeds	*Sasive beeja*	¼tsp	Omega 3, calcium, vitamin A & E, protein
Red chilli	*Kempu mensinakai*	1	Rich in flavonoids
Oil	*Taila*	1tsp	

Method

1. Heat ½ teaspoon oil in a frying pan. Add coriander seeds, cumin seeds and black pepper.
2. Add chopped dill leaves and green chilies. Fry until leaves are soft.
3. Add grated coconut, mix well and switch off the stove.
4. After the ingredients are cool, add required water and grind to a fine paste.
5. Transfer it to a pot and add one litre of water, tamarind extract, salt and jaggery (optional).
6. Bring it to a boil and temper it with oil, red chilli and mustard seeds.

Makes 4 cups. It is a refreshing soup.

Sapna was married into a very orthodox Rajasthani family. She had to slog it out the whole day doing chores and taking care of her family members. When she got pregnant, she hardly paid any attention to her own health and diet. Thankfully, she had a healthy baby, but she was very weak post delivery.

After her delivery, when she visited her mother's house, her mom was dismayed seeing her daughter in such a condition. With the help of her traditional wisdom, she started feeding her a diet rich in macro- as well micronutrients.

Post-delivery, Rajasthani women consume a calorie-rich diet with special emphasis on ghee and sugar. In some families no salt is consumed for the first six days and for the first three of those days, no grains. They believe this heals the tissues faster, though today, with medications and antibiotics, this approach looks a bit far-fetched.

RAJASTHAN

Gond Ke Ladoo (Edible Gum Ladoo)

L

Natural edible gum (ghatti gum) is believed to be beneficial during lactation. Most of the Rajasthani recipes include this ingredient. It is generally given after 10 days of delivery, for 2 weeks. It is also prepared in the form of gond ki rai and gond ki laapach.

Ingredients

 1 ladoo 

164kcal

English	Hindi	Amount	Use
Natural edible gum	*Gond*	20gm	Anti-oxidant, reduces lipids levels, complex carbohydrate
Almonds	*Badam*	15gm	Protein, magnesium and vitamin E
Pistachio	*Pista*	7gm	Rich in coenzyme Q10
Black pepper powder	*Kaali mirch*	5gm	Metabolic booster and anti-inflammatory
Amaranth flour	*Rajgirah atta*	50gm	High in protein, vitamin A, iron
Sugar	*Bura*	50gm	
Ghee	*Ghee*	3tbsp	Good source of fat

Method

1. Fry edible gum in 1 tablespoon of ghee. When it puffs up add the almonds and pistachios and sauté a bit.
2. Then roast the flour in 1 tablespoon ghee and when slightly brown, remove from heat and add the powdered nut and edible gum to it and mix.
3. Mix all the ingredients together.
4. Add heated ghee and make into ladoos.

Makes 6 ladoos of 20-25gm each (lemon-sized).

Sauth Ki Moi (Dry Ginger and Wheat Mix)

Sauth Ki Moi (Dry Ginger and Wheat Mix)

L

Ginger is soaked overnight in cow's milk, mashed and dried in the morning. It is then fried in ghee and made into a powder.

Ingredients

 ½ cup  242kcal

English	Hindi	Amount	Use
Wheat flour	*Gehun atta*	3tbsp	Macronutrients
Dry ginger powder	*Sauth*	2tsp	Helps in blood circulation, aids to relieve headache and migraine , anti-inflammatory
Almonds (crushed)	*Badam*	7-8 pcs.	Protein, magnesium and vitamin E
Sugar	*Bura*	2tbsp	
Ghee	*Ghee*	3tbsp	Good source of fat

Method

1. Roast flour and crushed almonds in ghee.
2. After it cools, add sauth powder and sugar.

Makes 1.5 cups. Instead of sugar, raisins can be added for sweetening the dish.

Geeli Haldi (Wet Turmeric)

Ingredients

1tsp  20kcal

English	Hindi	Amount	Use
Fresh turmeric	*Haldi*	250gm	Anti-microbial
Black pepper	*Kali mirch*	½tsp	Metabolic booster and anti-inflammatory
Salt	*Namak*	To taste	
Ghee	*Ghee*	1tbsp	Good source of fat

Method

1. Sauté the turmeric root (slit in long strands) in ghee and add salt and pepper to it.

Makes 1.5 cups. Consume within 7 days.

Haldi Ladoo (Turmeric Ladoo)

L

Turmeric has antibacterial, anti-fungal, anti-inflammatory properties due to its curcumin content. It helps in the healing of wounds, strengthens the bones and relieves cough and cold. Laddoos made of turmeric are given to mothers as part of post-natal care.

Ingredients

1 ladoo

158kcal

English	Hindi	Amount	Use
Natural edible gum	*Gond*	10gm	Anti-oxidant, complex carbohydrate. Reduces lipid levels
Almonds	*Badam*	15gm	Protein, magnesium and vitamin E
Turmeric	*Haldi*	50gm	Anti-microbial
Poppy seeds	*Khus khus*	10gm	Rich calcium source, immunity booster
Black pepper powder	*Kaali mirch*	5gm	Metabolic booster and anti-inflammatory
Whole wheat flour	*Gehun atta*	50gm	Macronutrients
Sugar	*Bura*	50gm	
Ghee	*Ghee*	3tbsp	Good source of fat

Method

1. Fry the edible gum till it puffs up. Sauté almonds, poppy seeds and powder all together.
2. Then roast the flour in ghee.
3. Combine all the ingredients together.
4. Heat rest of the ghee, add to the mixture and make ladoos.

Makes 6 lemon-sized ladoos. Eat one ladoo per day as a snack. Can swap sugar with dry fruits or jaggery.

Kankari Ajwain (Carrom Seeds Mix)

L

Carom seeds (ajwain) are believed to relieve gas and improve digestion. It also clears the uterine lining. The following recipe is supposed to purify blood apart from being a good appetite stimulant and back pain reliever. It also has a high protein and fibre content.

Ingredients

 1tsp 

79kcal

English	Hindi	Amount	Use
Carom seeds	*Ajwain*	5gm	Aids digestion, beats flatulence
Almonds (crushed)	*Badam*	5gm	Protein, magnesium and vitamin E
Jaggery/Sugar	*Gur/bura*	10gm	Rich in iron
Ghee	*Ghee*	1tbsp	Good source of fat
Natural edible gum	*Gond*	5gm	Anti-oxidant, complex carbohydrate. Reduces lipids levels
Dry coconut	*Giri*	3gm	Rich in vitamin E and essential fatty acids
Turmeric powder	*Haldi*	2 pinch	Anti-microbial
Choti peepal	*Choti peepal*	2 pinch	
False black pepper	*Vavding*	1 pinch	Aids digestion

Method

1. Fry the edible gum.
2. Sauté ajwain in ghee.
3. Add all the ingredients and mix.

Makes 1 tablespoon. Good to munch after food.

Supari Ladoo (Areca Nut Ladoo)

L

Areca nut is supposed to help the uterus shrink back to its size. It also strengthens the nerves. It stimulates the appetite and is also rich in magnesium. This ladoo is given after 40 days of delivery as the child may form more mucous secretions if given earlier.

Ingredients

 1 ladoo 

164kcal

English	Hindi	Amount	Use
Areca nut	*Chikni supari*	125gm	Helps to get rid of stomach worms, helps in uterus shrinking back to its original size
Cow's milk	*Dudh*	750ml	Rich source of protein, calcium and vitamins
Sugar	*Shakkar*	300gm	
Ghee	*Ghee*	50gm	Good source of fat
Saffron	*Kesar*	1.25gm	Boosts haemoglobin and stabilises mood
Masala			
Caraway seeds	*Shahi jeera*	2.5gm	Digestive health
Black pepper	*Kali mirch*	2.5gm	Metabolic booster and anti-inflammatory
Nutmeg	*Jaiphal*	2.5gm	Soothes nerves, reduces tension and anxiety
Mace	*Javitri*	2.5gm	Alleviates depression, improves digestion, improves blood circulation, releases serotonin
Long pepper	*Peepal*	2.5gm	Helps uterus to return to normal size
Dry ginger powder	*Sauth*	2.5gm	Helps in blood circulation, aids in relieving headache and migraine
Almonds	*Badam*	2.5gm	Protein, magnesium and vitamin E
Cardamom	*Elaichi*	2.5gm	Antacid
Sparrow grass	*Shatavar*	12.50gm	Rejuvenates female reproductive system
Chiroli seeds (seeds from *Buchanania lanzan* tree)	*Chiraunji*	2.5gm	Removes blood impurities
Clove	*Lavang*	2.5gm	Dental health and digestion
Sandalwood	*Chandan*	2.5gm	Has cooling properties
Coriander seeds	*Dhaniya*	2.5gm	High in calcium, aids digestion
Cumin seeds	*Jeera*	2.5gm	Aids digestion
Water chestnut flour	*Singhara*	5gm	High in protein, vitamin A, iron

Ingredients (...conti)

English	Hindi	Amount	Use
Nut grass	*Nagarmotha*	2.5gm	Reduces breast soreness
Indian gooseberry powder	*Dry amla powder*	2.5gm	High in vitamin C
Indian rose chestnut	*Nag kesar*	2.5gm	Anti-inflammatory and reduces depression
Snake cucumber seeds	*Kakadi seeds*	2.5gm	Removes blood impurities
Spiny bamboo	*Vanslochan*	2.5gm	Anti-diarrheal
Bark of lodhra tree *(Symplocos racemosa)*	*Lodh*	2.5gm	Increase female hormones (FSH, LH). Good for uterine health
Bay leaf	*Tej patta*	0.25gm	Rich in phytonutrients

Method

1. Grind the areca nut and sieve it and make a powder.
2. Reduce milk and areca nut powder in a thick bottomed pan until it becomes thick.
3. Grind all the masala and sieve it.
4. Then take ghee in a pan and sauté the paste made of areca nut and milk till golden brown, then add all the masalas.
5. After it cools down, add sugar and saffron and make into small balls.

Makes 15 ladoos of 25gm each. The sugar can be replaced with jaggery and the quantity can be reduced.

Dashmool Kada (Herbal Decoction)

Ingredients

 ½ glass  25kcal

English	Hindi	Amount	Use
Malay beechwood	*Shaulpardni (sewan)*	10gm	Antioxidant, treatment of vaginal discharge
Dabra (*Uraria picta*)	*Pashnipardni (pithvan)*	10gm	Analgesic
Yellow-berried nightshade	*Choti kateri*	10gm	Prevents accumulation of excessive fluid in tissues
Forest bitterberry	*Badi kateri*	10gm	Treats scanty menses
Land caltrops	*Gokhru*	10gm	Treatment of female disorders, increases physical strength
Indian bael *(Aegle marmelos)*	*Belmool (chaal)*	10gm	Anti-bacterial
Indian trumpet	*Shyonak (chaal)*	10gm	Carminative
Creek premna	*Arni (chaal)*	10gm	Strengthens bones
Gmelina	*Gambhari (chaal)*	10gm	Anti-inflammatory
Fragrant rose flower	*Paatla (chaal)*	10gm	Neuro protective and hepato protective
Dry ginger powder	*Sauth*	2.5gm	Helps in blood circulation, aids to relieve headache and migraine
Almonds	*Badam*	2.5gm	Protein, magnesium and vitamin E
Cardamom	*Elaichi*	2.5gm	Antacid
Sparrow grass	*Shatavar*	12.50gm	Rejuvenates female reproductive system
Chiroli seeds (seeds from *Buchanania lanzan* tree)	*Chiraunji*	2.5gm	Removes blood impurities
Clove	*Lavang*	2.5gm	Dental health & digestion

Method

1. Mix all the ingredients and divide them in 10 parts.
2. Soak overnight 1 part in 1 glass of water in a brass vessel (during winters) or in mud pots (during summer), boil it and bring it to half the volume.
3. Add 1 teaspoon honey and drink.

Battissa Kada (Herbal Decoction)

L

It helps in alleviating fever. Aids in digestion and relieves gas. This mixture is also readily available.

Ingredients

 2 litres over the day. 

10kcal

English	Hindi	Amount	Use
Sugar	*Sakkar*	30gm	
*	*Naarkaata*	21.5gm	
Liquorice	*Mulethi*	20gm	Hormonal balance
Dry ginger	*Sauth*	15gm	Anti-inflammatory
Bark of lodhra tree (*Symplocos racemosa*)	*Lodh*	15gm	Increases female hormones (FSH, LH)
Indian ginseng	*Ashwagandha*	12.5gm	Anti-depressant
Black musli	*Kaali musli*	12.5gm	Tonic
Mountain knot grass	*Bui kaltan*	12.5gm	Memory enhancer
Indian sarsaparilla	*Anant mool*	12.5gm	Diuretic
Land caltrops	*Gokhru*	10.5gm	Treatment of female health disorders, increases physical strength
Velvet bean	*Kaunch bheej*	7.5gm	Neuroprotective
Carom seeds	*Ajwain*	7.5gm	Aids digestion, beats flatulence
Psyllium husk	*Isabgol*	5gm	Soluble fibre
Areca nut	*Supari*	5gm	Helps to get rid of stomach worms
*	*Ghiya pathar*	500gm	
Black pepper	*Kaali mirch*	2.5gm	Metabolic booster and anti-inflammatory
Black cardamon	*Badi elaichi*	2.5gm	Oral health
Lotus seeds	*Talmakhana*	2.5gm	Helps repair damaged proteins
Basil seeds	*Tulsi seeds*	2.5gm	Normalizes cortisol
Nutmeg	*Jaiphal*	1.25gm	Soothes nerves, reduces tension and anxiety
China root (*Smilax chinensis*)	*Chopchini*	1.25gm	Antipyretic
Rose petals	*Gulab kali*	1.25gm	Cleanses liver and gall bladder
Pelitory	*Akalkara*	1.25gm	Lessens edema and swelling
Shorea robusta	*Saalam mishri*	0.60gm	Analgesic
Indian spider plant	*Safed musli*	0.6gm	Improves the function of reproductive organs
*	*Panjab misri*	0.6gm	

* English equivalent unknown

Ingredients (...conti)

English	Hindi	Amount	Use
*	*Kathali gond*	5gm	
Piper longum	*Pipramul*	5gm	Improves blood circulation by inhibiting platelet aggregation, acts as a digestive stimulant and an immunomodulatory
Spiny bamboo	*Vanslochan*	5gm	Antidiarrheal
Chinese garlic	*Bakeri*	5gm	Analgesic
Climbing lang-lang	*Madanmast*	5gm	Antifungal
Indian rose chestnut	*Nag kesar*	5gm	Anti-inflammatory and reduces depression
False black pepper	*Vavding*	5gm	Aids digestion
Chebulic myrobalan	*Harad*	5gm	Laxative effect
Berillic myrobalans	*Behada*	5gm	Effective for headache
Tomentosa babool	*Babliya ki phali*	5gm	Good for treating hair fall
Pomegrenate	*Anaar*	5gm	Immunity booster
Bayleaf	*Tejpatta*	2.5gm	Rich in phytonutrients
Sacred fig	*Choti peepal*	2.5gm	Anti-inflammatory, multiple uses
Bastard teak	*Kamarkas*	2.5gm	To strengthen the lower back

* English equivalent unknown

Method

1. Grind all the ingredients and divide in 32 parts.
2. Then boil one part in 2 litres of water in a brass container and strain it.
3. Drink it during the whole day, sip by sip.

Laud Ladoo

It has a cooling effect on the body and also good for the eyes and brain.

Ingredients

 1 ladoo 

175kcal

English	Hindi	Amount	Use
Bark of Lodhra tree *(Symplocos racemosa)*	*Laud powder*	50gm	Boosts female hormones (FSH, LH)
Water chestnut flour	*Singhara atta*	250gm	High in protein, vitamin A, iron
Edible gum	*Gond*	50gm	Anti- oxidant, complex carbohydrate. Reduces lipids levels
Almonds (crushed)	*Badam*	100gm	Protein, magnesium and vitamin E
Dry coconut (crushed)	*Giri*	100gm	Rich in vitamin E
Sugar powder	*Shakkar*	250gm	
Black pepper	*Kaali mirch*	25gm	Metabolic booster and anti-inflammatory
Ghee	*Ghee*	250gm	Good source of fat

Method

1. Sauté almond, laud, water chestnut flour, gum and dry coconut, all separately in ghee.
2. Mix all the ingredients with sugar.
3. Heat ghee, add to the mixture and make ladoos.

Makes 30 lemon-sized ladoos. It is usually given one-and-a-half months after childbirth and mostly in the summer months only.

Pipramul Milk

L

Long pepper is generally given after 4-5 days of delivery. It increases heat in the body, increases blood circulation, promotes sound sleep and relieves headache. It may lead to sweating. The powder should be given with milk at night.

Ingredients

 ¾ cup 

177kcal

English	Hindi	Amount	Use
Long pepper	*Pipramul*	6gm	Improves blood circulation by inhibiting platelet aggregation, digestive stimulant
Cow's milk	*Dudh*	250ml	Rich source of protein, calcium and vitamins
Almond	*Badam*	10 pcs.	Protein, magnesium and vitamin E
Betel leaves	*Paan*	2	Rich source of magnesium. Increases milk production
Sugar	*Mishri*	15gm	

Method

1. Long pepper powder is mixed with warm milk and taken.
2. After that, betel leaf with almond and sugar is given.

Makes a little more than a cup.

Khaskhas Ladoo (Poppy Seed Ladoo)

L

Poppy seeds are a rich source of calcium and helps in lactation. It can be taken after soaking in water overnight and making a paste, which is then sautéed in ghee. It can also be made in the form of ladoo. It is a good snack option.

Ingredients

 1 ladoo 

147kcal

English	Hindi	Amount	Use
Poppy seeds	*Khaskhas*	15gm	Rich calcium source, Immunity booster
Water chestnut flour	*Singhara atta*	50gm	High in protein, vitamin A, iron
Edible gum	*Gond*	10gm	Anti-oxidant, complex carbohydrate. Reduces lipids levels
Almonds crushed	*Badam*	15gm	Protein, magnesium and vitamin E
Dry coconut crushed	*Giri*	25gm	Rich in vitamin E
Sugar powder	*Shakkar*	50gm	
Muskmelon seeds	*Kharbuza ke beej*	15gm	Galactagogue
Black pepper	*Kaali mirch*	5gm	Metabolic booster and anti-inflammatory
Ghee	*Ghee*	15gm	Good source of fat

Method

1. Soak poppy seeds and melon seeds for 12 hours, after dry roasting it slightly in a hot pan.
2. Grind to a paste.
3. Fry the edible gum in ghee and powder it.
4. Sauté the almonds and water chestnut flour in ghee.
5. Combine all the ingredients with heated ghee and make ladoos.

Makes 8 lemon-sized ladoos.

Paan Masala (Herbs with Betel Leaves)

L

Two betel leaves to be consumed after breakfast and lunch. Betel leaves improve energy levels and are rich sources of magnesium.

Ingredients

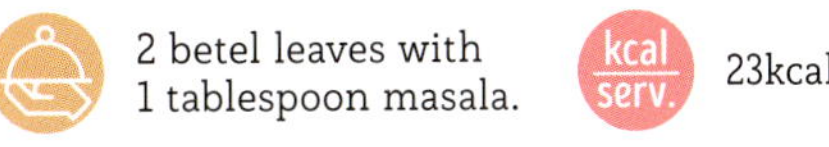

English	Hindi	Amount	Use
Areca nut	*Chikni supari*	500gm	Helps to get rid of stomach worms
Liquorice	*Mulethi*	375gm	Restore hormonal balance
Black cardamom	*Badi elaichi*	125gm	Oral health
Cardamom	*Choti elaichi*	50gm	Digestive health
Catechu	*Katha*	125gm	Antibacterial
Lime	*Choona*	50gm	Calcium
Almonds	*Badam*	125gm	Protein, magnesium and vitamin E
Coriander	*Dhaniya goli*	250gm	Indigestion
Clove	*Lavang*	25gm	For dental health and digestion
Fennel seeds	*Saunf*	250gm	Anti-flatulent
Ghee	*Ghee*	2tsp	Good source of fat
Peppermint	*Pudina*	2gm	Headache

Method

1. Sauté all the ingredients except catechu and lime.
2. Make a coarse masala of all the ingredients.
3. Put little of this masala in the betel leaf (Kapuri paan).
4. Can add ajwain also.

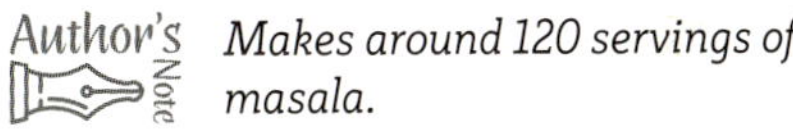

Makes around 120 servings of masala.

Mishiti, a Bengali by birth, married into an Oriya family. She had a very healthy lifestyle. Bengalis have a unique and distinct taste in cuisine. She was a real foodie, so adapting to the culinary culture of Orissa was not an issue with her. But when she got pregnant, all she craved was for Bengali food. Though there is a lot of similarities between Bengali and Oriya cuisine, the preparation methods are quite different. For instance, post-delivery, poppy seeds are given to the lactating mother in both the cultures but the way it is prepared is different. Bengalis mostly avoid egg in the initial days as it is believed to cause increased flatulence. Chicken is consumed only in the form of stews. Fish is preferred during this time. Here are a few recipes of postpartum foods among Bengalis.

A rich custom and set of belief prevails among the people residing in India's northeastern states, which comprises the states of Arunachal Pradesh, Assam, Manipur, Mizoram, Meghalaya, Nagaland and Tripura.

Being the organic part of India, it has an enormous stretch of zone producing a wide array of fruits and vegetables. Their post-pregnancy diet consists of their staple food—rich, fresh water fish and vegetables.

BENGAL, ODISHA & NORTHEASTERN STATES

Shukto (Mixed Vegetable in Poppy Seed Paste)

L

Drumstick is a very nutrition-dense food. It acts like an antibiotic. It is a rich source of vitamins, minerals, proteins and anti-oxidants. It is generally included in any vegetable and pulse preparation given to the nursing mother

Poppy seeds are used widely because of their rich calcium content and galactagogue properties. It is soaked overnight, ground into a paste and is sautéed in ghee.

Ingredients

1 cup

257kcal

English	Bengali	Amount	Use
Drumstick	*Dhaker kathi*	1 pc.	Antibacterial
Potato	*Aloo*	1 pc.	High potassium content
Bitter gourd	*Tikta lau*	1 p.c	Antidiabetic
Raw banana	*Kasa kola*	1 pc.	Serotonin
French beans	*Pharasi*	100gm	Dietary fibre
Mustard paste	*Sariso*	25gm	Omega 3, vitamin A, calcium and protein
Ginger paste	*Adaa*	25gm	Anti-inflammatory
Mustard oil	*Sariso tel*	1tbsp	Omega 3 rich
Poppy seed paste	*Postadana*	25gm	High in calcium
Black mustard	*Kaloo sarisa*	1tsp	Decongestant
Ghee	*Ghee*	1tsp	Good source of fat
Salt	*Labon*	To taste	

Method

1. Cut and wash the vegetables.
2. Put the pieces in turmeric water.
3. Heat mustard oil in a pan.
4. Add black mustard and the ginger paste.
5. Cook until it becomes golden brown.
6. Add mustard paste, poppy seed paste and turmeric.
7. Cook until the oil separates.
8. Then add the vegetables and sauté for 2 minutes.
9. Add water and cook until the vegetables are tender.
10. Add 1 teaspoon ghee on top and the dish is ready to serve.

Makes 2 cups.

Rui Macher Jhol (Rui Fish in Gravy)

Ingredients

 1 cup 

269kcal

English	Bengali	Amount	Use
Rui fish	*Ruimaas*	500gm	High in iron
Potato	*Aloo*	100gm	High in potassium
Shallot	*Gandho pyaaz*	50gm	High allicin content, antioxidant, anti-inflammatory
Bay leaves	*Teja pata*	2	Anti-flatulence
Peppercorn	*Marib*	1tbsp	Metabolic booster
Ginger paste	*Adaa*	1tsp	Anti-inflammatory
Cumin powder	*Jeera*	1tsp	Rich in thymol which increases milk
Turmeric powder	*Halud*	1tsp	Anti-inflammatory
Salt	*Labon*	To taste	
Mustard oil	*Sariso tel*	2tbsp	Omega 3
Nigella seeds	*Kalojeera*	1/2tsp	Improves immunity

Method

1. Fry the fish and keep aside.
2. Add bay leaves and peppercorn in that hot pan. Add all the vegetables and sauté for some time. Add nigella seeds, ginger paste, turmeric and cumin powder, stir a little, add salt.
3. After a few minutes, add fish and hot water, let it cook on high flame for a few minutes, and simmer until it is cooked well, for about 5 to 10 minutes.
4. The fish stew is ready.

Makes 3 cups. This dish is protein rich, each serving providing 33 grams of protein.

Mochar Ghonto (Banana Flower and Potato)

Ingredients

 1 cup 

133kcal

English	Bengali	Amount	Use
Banana flower	*Mochar tarkari*	1	Balances hormones
Potato	*Aloo*	1	High in potassium
Bay leaves	*Teja pata*	2	Anti-flatulent
Fresh coconut	*Nariyal*	¼ cup	The high lauric acid contents give antibacterial, anti-inflammatory and antiviral properties
Garlic	*Rasuna*	4 pcs.	High allicin content
Ginger paste	*Adaa*	1tsp	Anti-inflammatory
Cumin	*Jeera*	½tsp	Thymol content improves lactation
Turmeric	*Halud*	¼tsp	Anti-inflammatory
Salt	*Labon*	To taste	
Ghee	*Ghee*	1tsp	Good source of fat
Mustard oil	*Sariso tel*	1tsp	Omega 3

Method

1. Pressure cook a cleaned and chopped banana flower with 1/2 cup water upto 2 whistles. Once cool, gently mash using the back of a ladle.
2. The next step is to make the curry. Heat a heavy-bottomed pan with mustard oil over low flame.
3. When the oil starts to smoke, add bay leaves and cumin seeds.
4. Now add ginger and garlic and sauté for 30 seconds.
5. Add potato cubes and cook till tender.
6. Once the potatoes are cooked and dry add the cooked banana blossom, and mix well. Cook covered for 2 minutes.
7. Adjust salt and add the grated fresh coconut.

Makes 2 cups.

Muri Ladoo (Puffed Riced Ladoo)

Sabudana Kheer (Tapioca Pearl Pudding)

Ingredients

 1 cup  202kcal

English	Bengali	Amount	Use
Tapioca/Sago pearls	*Sabudana*	½ cup (soaked)	High in fibre, iron and B-Complex vitamins
Cow's milk	*Dudh*	2 cups	High in calcium, vitamins and protein
Sugar	*Chini*	3tbsp	

Method

1. Soak tapioca pearls for some time and then rinse till it is cleared of starch.
2. Put milk on medium heat and add the tapioca pearls, stirring occasionally.
3. Add sugar and cook for 3-4 minutes.
4. Dry fruits, cardamom is also added to increase its nutritional value.

Makes about 2.5 cups. Sugar can be replaced with dry fruits.

Muri Ladoo (Puffed Rice Ladoo)

Bengalis use date palm jaggery known as 'khejur gur' because it is very high in iron.

Ingredients

 1 ladoo  134kcal

English	Bengali	Amount	Use
Puffed rice	*Muri*	250gm	B-Complex vitamins
Water		3 cups	
Date palm jaggery	*Khejur gur*	750gm	Rich in iron

Method

1. Place jaggery and water in a pan and dissolve the jaggery over low heat.
2. Once the jaggery dissolves, increase the heat and bring it to boil and cook over full flame till a two-thread consistency is reached.
3. Mix in the puffed rice quickly into the mixture.
4. Take it off the heat and let it cool for a while.
5. Make round balls or squares, moistening the hands if it feels sticky.

Makes 30 golf-ball-sized ladoos.

Uttar Pradesh is a large state with a vibrant food culture consisting of both vegetarian and non-vegetarian cuisines. Eighty-three percent of the population live in villages. There are widespread instances of early marriage and multiple pregnancies.

When Sadhna, who hails from a UP Brahmin family in Varanasi, got pregnant, she was elated that she could now eat all her favorite dishes, especially the sweets. Sadhna realized that there were a lot of beliefs and practices related to pregnancy, mainly in the villages. For instance, the villagers believed that the pregnant woman has to eat less as she nears the due date so that the baby does not grow big and make the delivery difficult. But her doctor advised her to eat healthy as she and the baby needed special care during this phase. In the villages, they first feed some honey, ghee and jaggery to the newborn before the first feed from the mother. These were all practices that Sadhna considered unscientific and decided to not follow them. She made a list of recipes she found with some sound reasoning and decided that she would make it a part of her pregnancy diet plan.

The following recipes are mostly prepared for good breast milk production, digestive health and to revitalize the body with good nutrition.

UTTAR PRADESH

Suthora (Fox Nut and Dry Fruit Ladoos)

It is an energy-dense ladoo which can be eaten anytime of the day.

Ingredients

 1 ladoo 

122kcal

English	Hindi	Amount	Use
Jaggery	*Desi gur*	200gm	Rich in iron
Cashew	*Kaju*	25gm	High in oleic acid & good for heart health
Almonds	*Badam*	25gm	Rich in protein and vitamin E
Fox nut	*Makhana*	25gm	Helps to repair damaged proteins
Dry coconut	*Giri*	50gm	Strengthens connective tissue
Poppy seeds	*Post dana*	10gm	Rich calcium source, immunity booster
Dates deseeded	*Chuwara*	50gm	Vitamin A,C,E & magnesium
Pistachio	*Pista*	10gm	Rich in coenzyme Q10
Raisins	*Kishmis*	50gm	Rich in iron
Ghee	*Ghee*	50gm	Good source of fat
Chiroli seeds (seeds from *Buchanania lanzan* tree)	*Chiraunji*	10gm	Removes blood impurities
Natural edible gum	*Gond*	25gm	Antioxidant, controls lipid levels, complex carbohydrate
Dry ginger	*Sauth*	10gm	Helps in blood circulation, aids to relieve headache and migraine

Method

1. Heat the ghee in a pan and fry the edible gum and nuts (cashew, almonds, fox nuts and pistachio), and grind them in a mixer after cooling it.
2. Then sauté the dry coconut and poppy seeds in low flame and add dry ginger, chiroli seeds, dates and raisins.
3. Melt the jaggery separately.
4. Mix all the ingredients to make ladoos.

Makes 15 lemon-sized ladoos.

Harira (Mixed Nuts Snack)

L

Harira is given 2-3 times a day as a snack during the first three days after childbirth.

Ingredients

English	Hindi	Amount	Use
Dry ginger powder	*Sonth*	¼tsp	Helps in blood circulation, aids to relieve headache and migraine
Carom seeds	*Ajwain*	1tbsp	Aids digestion, beats flatulence
Cumin seeds	*Jeera*	½tbsp	Thymol, which increases milk
Turmeric powder	*Haldi*	½tbsp	Anti-inflammatory
Mixed nuts	*Badam* *Kaju* *Akhrot*	50gm	Rich in micro-nutrients
Jaggery/Sugar	*Gur/Shakkar*	40gm	Rich in iron
Ghee	*Ghee*	50gm	Good source of fat

Method

1. Powder the nuts, pour ghee in a pan and sauté in low flame.
2. Add the rest of the ingredients and sauté for few seconds.
3. Then add water and jaggery to make a paste of a very loose consistency.

Makes 3 cups. Quantity of sugar can be reduced. Limit consumption to once in a day.

Makhana Kheer (Fox Nut and Milk Pudding)

Makhana Kheer (Fox Nut and Milk Pudding)

Ingredients

 1 cup  206kcal

English	Hindi	Amount	Use
Milk	*Doodh*	1 litre	Rich source of protein, calcium and vitamins
Dates	*Chuwara*	10 pcs.	Vitamin A,C,E & magnesium
Almonds	*Badam*	25gm	Rich in protein and vitamin E
Fox nut	*Makhana*	25gm	Helps repair damaged proteins

Method

1. Grind the almonds and dates together.
2. Put all the ingredients in a pan and simmer on the gas till the quantity reduces to half and serve hot.

Author's Note: *Makes 5 cups.*

Ajwain Water (Carrom Seed Water)

This water is prepared once and sipped through the day.

Ingredients

 1 litre for the day  Negligible

English	Hindi	Amount	Use
Water	*Paani*	3 litre	
Carrom seeds	*Ajwain*	15gm	Aids digestion, beats flatulence
Asafoetida	*Hing*	1gm	Relieves gas

Method

1. Make a packet of asafoetida and carom seeds in a muslin cloth.
2. Put it in the vessel with the water and boil it for 10 minutes.

Author's Note: *Makes 3 litres. Relieves gas and indigestion.*

Buknoo Churan (Digestive Herb Mix)

This is given after 6-7 days of delivery to aid in digestion and relieve acidity.

Ingredients

 1tsp  Negligible

English	Hindi	Amount	Use
Dry turmeric root	*Haldi jad*	25gm	Antimicrobial
Rock salt	*Sendha namak*	10gm	
Black salt	*Kaala namak*	10gm	
Long pepper	*Peepri*	10gm	Helps uterus to return to normal size
Piper longum	*Pipramul*	10gm	Improves blood circulation by inhibiting platelet aggregation, digestive stimulant and immunomodulatory
Dry ginger	*Sauth*	10gm	Helps in blood circulation, aids to relieve headache and migraine
Carrom seeds	*Ajwain*	10gm	Aids digestion, beats flatulence
Chebulic myrobalan	*Harad*	10gm	Antibacterial
Black pepper	*Kaali mirch*	10gm	Metabolic booster and anti-inflammatory
Mustard oil	*Sarson tel*	5gm	Rich in omega 3

Method

1. Heat mustard oil in a pan and roast turmeric root and Chebulic myrobalan.
2. Allow it to cool.
3. Add the rest of the ingredients and grind to form a powder.

Makes around 100gm of churan. Take 1 teaspoon after any meal.

Divya was getting ready for her *pulikuti* (literally meaning 'drinking tamarind juice') which is a pregnancy ceremony of the Nair community. It is performed on a particular day in the ninth month of pregnancy, at a time fixed by the local astrologer. Her Ammayi or maternal uncle's wife and her brother would be conducting this ceremony. Her Ammayi was an experienced hand. She had a long chat with Divya about some medicinal oils and herbs used during this period..

Kerala is well-known for its ayurvedic massages. One of Divya's friends in fact had taken a complete "prasava raksha" package from the famous Kottakkal Arya Vaidya Sala. But Divya wasn't planning to do that. She had the whole pregnancy plan laid out. Her daily ritual for the next three months would be a hot oil massage with Balaswagandhadi Taila, Ksheerabala Taila or Bala Taila to help strengthen her lower back and hip muscles and tendons. She had already ordered for some preparations like Dashamoolarishtam, which she has to take for two months after childbirth as it helps relieve pain and inflammation, Jeerakarishtam to be taken during the rainy season to keep the body warm and Shatavari Gulam to achieve hormonal balance. Her friend told her about the Pulilehyam to be taken from the third week of delivery for a month.

She is looking forward to tasting the Uluva Lehyam. She had heard it was delicious. The Pookkula Lehyam is made from the delicate tender coconut flowers and loads of coconut milk that is revered by Keralites. These flowers are the most prominent object in elegant Malayali weddings; they are a symbol of fertility.

Preceding the monsoon in Kerala is the mango season. What better way to use raw mangoes than making the Manga Chammandi. The well-balanced sour and pungent components titillate your taste buds. Divya mixed this with hot rice and savoured it all through her third trimester as it coincided with the raw mango season by chance.

KERALA

Manga Chammandi (Raw Mango Chutney)

To be mixed with hot rice and served. Goes well with curd rice too.

Ingredients

 1tbsp 

33kcal

English	Malayalam	Amount	Use
Raw mango (skin removed)	*Maanga*	½ of one	Rich in vitamins A and E. Also enriches the hormonal system
Shallots	*Cheriya ulli*	5	Rich source of potassium, increases production of master antioxidant glutathione
Grated coconut	*Thenga*	4-5tbsp	Rich in vitamin E and essential fatty acids required for growth of the baby during pregnancy
Green chillies	*Pachamulaku*	3	Rich in antioxidants
Red chilli powder	*Mulakupodi*	To taste	Rich in antioxidants
Grated ginger	*Inji*	½tsp	Aids digestion

Method

1. Grind all the raw ingredients together without adding water. Add required amount of salt as per taste.

Makes around 10 tablespoons.

Muringaila Curry (Drumstick Leaf Curry)

Ingredients

 1 cup  131kcal

English	Malayalam	Amount	Use
Drumstick leaf	*Murungaila*	1 cup	Rich in iron, vitamins, zinc, calcium and iron. Boosts lactation
Coconut scrapings	*Thenga*	½ cup	Rich in vitamin E and essential fatty acids required for the growth of the baby during pregnancy
Garlic	*Veluthulli*	6-8 cloves	Antifungal, helps maintain milk supply in breasts and helps avoid mastitis in breastfeeding moms
Cumin seeds	*Jeeragam*	1tsp	Aids in digestion
Green chillies	*Pachamulaku*	2	Rich in antioxidants
Curry leaves	*Kariveppila*	10 leaves	Rich in vitamins, minerals and antioxidants
Red chilli powder	*Mulakupodi*	As required	Rich in antioxidants

Method

1. Grind coconut, garlic, cumin, green chillies and curry leaves into a fine paste.
2. Add water into this smooth paste and make a gravy.
3. Allow the gravy to boil after adding the finely cut drumstick leaves.
4. Add a pinch of red chilli powder and salt as per taste requirements.
5. Bring the curry to just one boil and switch off the heat.

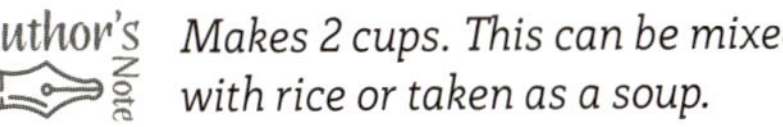

Makes 2 cups. This can be mixed with rice or taken as a soup.

Lehyam (Tender Coconut Flower Halwa)

 1 square inch piece  182kcal

Amount	Use
1	Energy booster, aids breast milk production, stops back pain
300ml	The high lauric acid contents give antibacterial, anti-inflammatory and antiviral properties
½tsp	Increases breast milk, aids digestion
¾tsp	Improves metabolic activity
1tsp	Anti-inflammatory
4tsp	Micronutrients rich
350gm	Increases alkalinity in the body, rich in iron
1 pinch	

7. Stir well and make sure that there are no lumps.
8. Switch on the flame and cook on medium heat, stirring continuously.
9. When half cooked, add the coconut milk-rice mix and cook till oil oozes out and is of halwa consistency.
10. Spread on a greased plate and cut into squares after cooling.

Makes 10 one-square inch pieces.

Uluva Lehyam (Fenugreek Halwa)

Ingredients

 ¼ cup  174kcal

English	Malayalam	Amount	Use
Fenugreek seeds	*Uluva*	100gm	Galactagogue
Thick coconut milk	*Onnaam thenga paal*	200ml	The high lauric acid contents give antibacterial, anti-inflammatory and antiviral properties
Cumin seeds	*Jeeragam*	1tsp	Contains digestive enzymes
Mustard seeds	*Kaduku*	1tsp	Good source of vitamin A and E, calcium
Turmeric powder	*Manjal podi*	1tsp	Anti-inflammatory
Salt	*Uppu*	1 pinch	
Roasted rice flour	*Puttu podi*	2tbsp	Micronutrients rich
Jaggery	*Vellam/sharkara*	450gm	Rich in iron, an immunity booster

Method

1. Soak cleaned fenugreek seeds for at least 4 hours.
2. Wash and pressure cook till done. After it cools, grind it to a slightly coarse consistency.
3. Dissolve the jaggery in 2 cups of boiling water and keep aside.
4. Make a paste of cumin, mustard seeds and turmeric by adding some water.
5. In a thick pan, add all the ingredients and stir continuously on medium heat.
6. Stir till a thick brownish mass is formed and starts leaving the sides of the pan.
7. Take it off the heat, pour it into a plate and level it.

Makes 3.5 cups.

While we intend to make the reader aware of the richness of our Indian diet and some of its ingredients, it is equally imperative to equip them with ideas to incorporate it into everyday life. As pregnant and lactating mothers are a special population and require the best in nutrition, it is very important to learn the tricks of balancing the old and the new values.

A plethora of information is available in these topics to cater to the demand as people are eager to find ways to improve their family's health. But it is very difficult to translate this eagerness into reasonable everyday practice.

A knowledgeable person may avoid greasy parathas and replace it with a bowl of cereal, which is packed with simple sugars. By missing out on traditional recipes we lose the advantage of a variety of ingredients rich in micronutrients.

More people are taking to processed foods due to lack of time, not realizing that they are depleted in nutrients.

The World Wide Web is flooded with diet plans that are more suited for the West. It hands out loads of information only about items available in plenty abroad—Broccoli, kiwi fruit, kale, avocado, etc., which are not only alien to our culture but also not very affordable or accessible. The net-surfing generation, being fed only those facts, is largely of the opinion that those are the only good sources of the nutrients. Information on our country's varied indigenous ingredients are not available easily. It can only be obtained through a conscious and informed search. Numerous research papers are being presented on these ingredients but hardly any come to the fore for the general public to be aware of their value and goodness.

WHERE TRADITION
MEETS SCIENCE
AND CONVENIENCE

Sample Diet During Pregnancy

These sample diets depict how a 2000kcal diet looks like. It is designed for woman within the pre-pregnancy weight range of 50-60kg. During the different stages of pregnancy the appetite may vary from person to person. The body might develop cravings for certain foods. Some may experience morning sickness, nausea or other complications like water retention. The intake should cater to

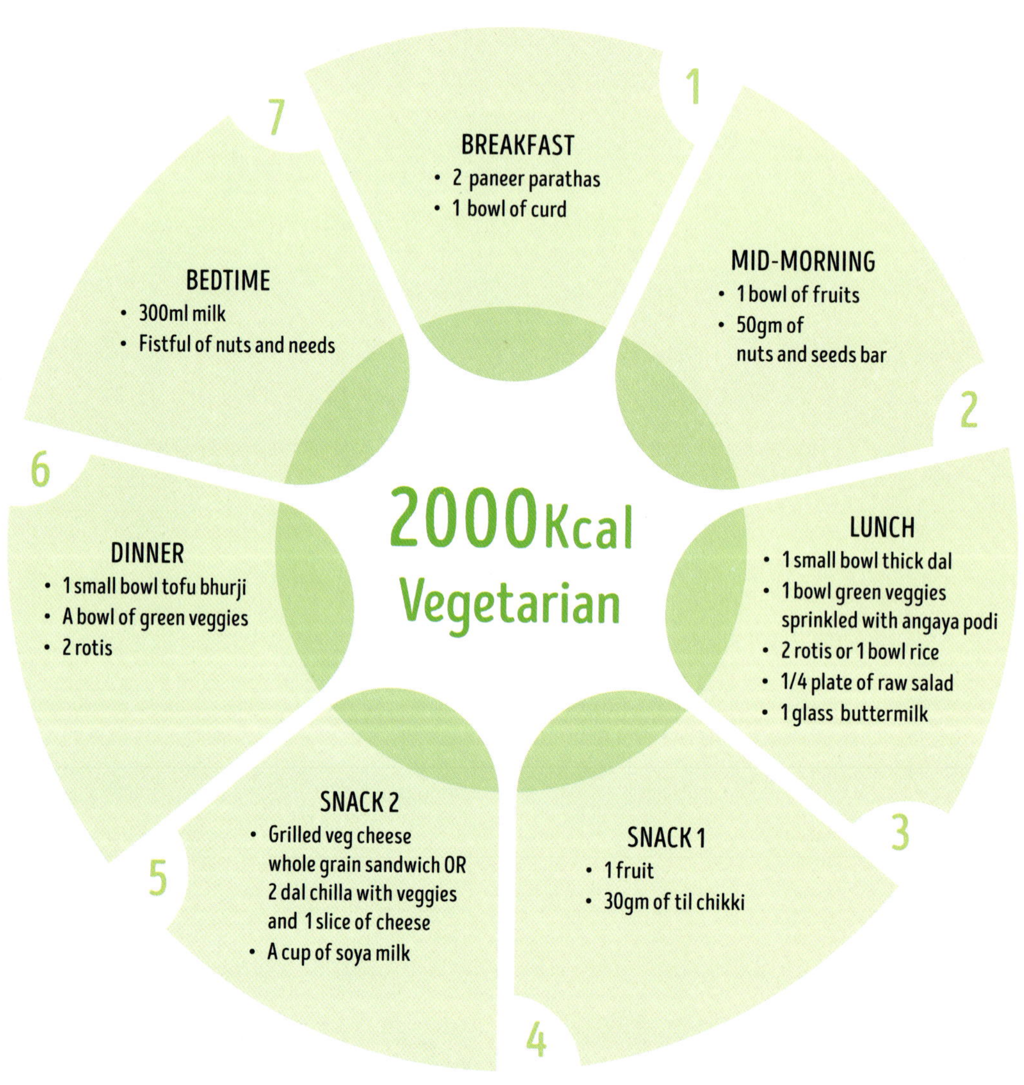

such changed preferences. Women with lactose intolerance or gluten sensitivity are not considered in this plan because a customized approach is required in such cases. It is best to add a lot of variety to the diet in the form of varied fruits, vegetables and wholesome grains and millets. Iron, calcium, folic acid rich recipes from snacks recipe section of the book can be incorporated in the diet plan as required.

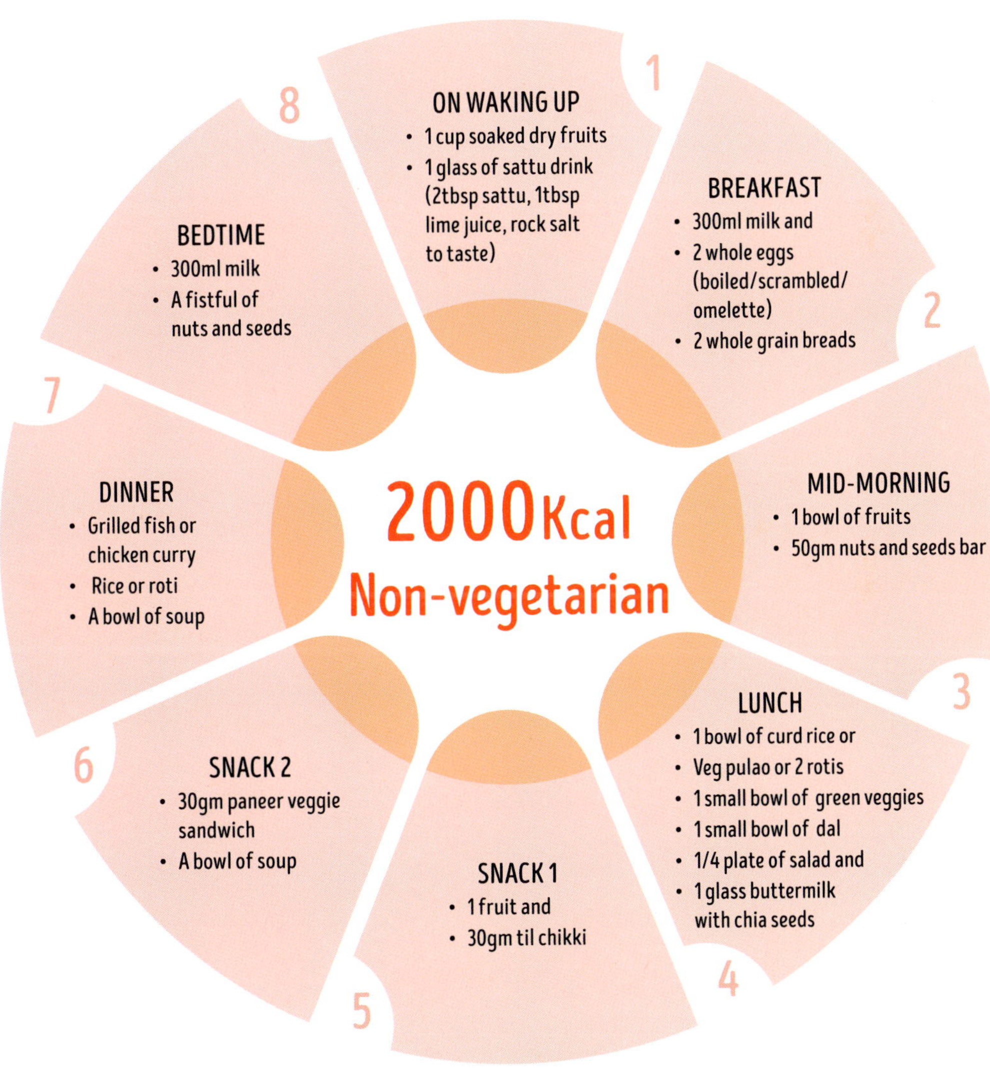

Sample Diet for Postpartum

Post-pregnancy is a very vital period where the body is replenishing all its nutrient stores and also aiming to provide the baby with a rich quality and quantity of breast milk which directly impacts the health of the infant. Here is a sample diet plan of 2350kcal. These plans include the best of the recipes from various states because of the quality and bio-availability of the nutrients in them and their role in increasing milk

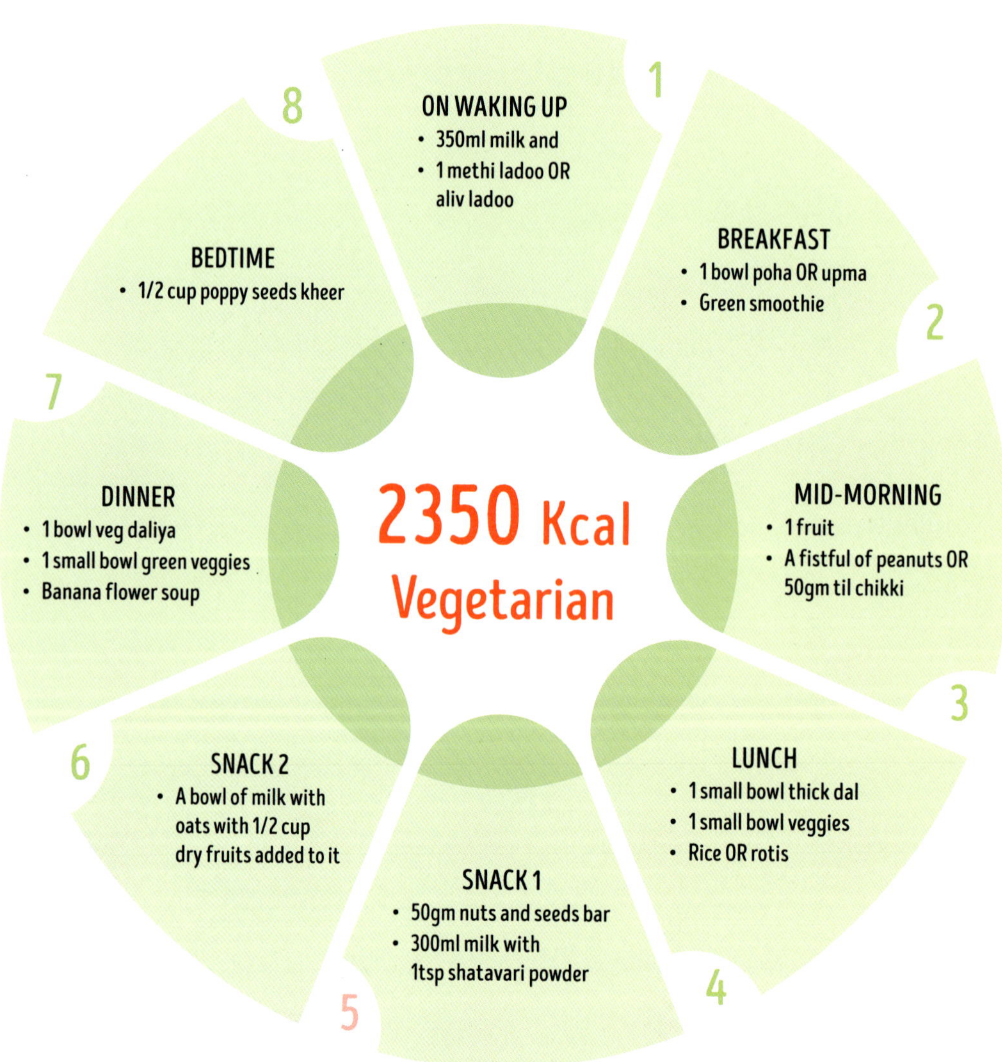

production. In the first few days of the post-delivery period it is advised to have a diet which is easily digestible and tolerable. It is best to go by the individual's body instincts as to what will suit since everyone has different symptoms and conditions.

This plan also equips you to incorporate the star ingredients in your diet which are so important to the vitality and immunity of your body.

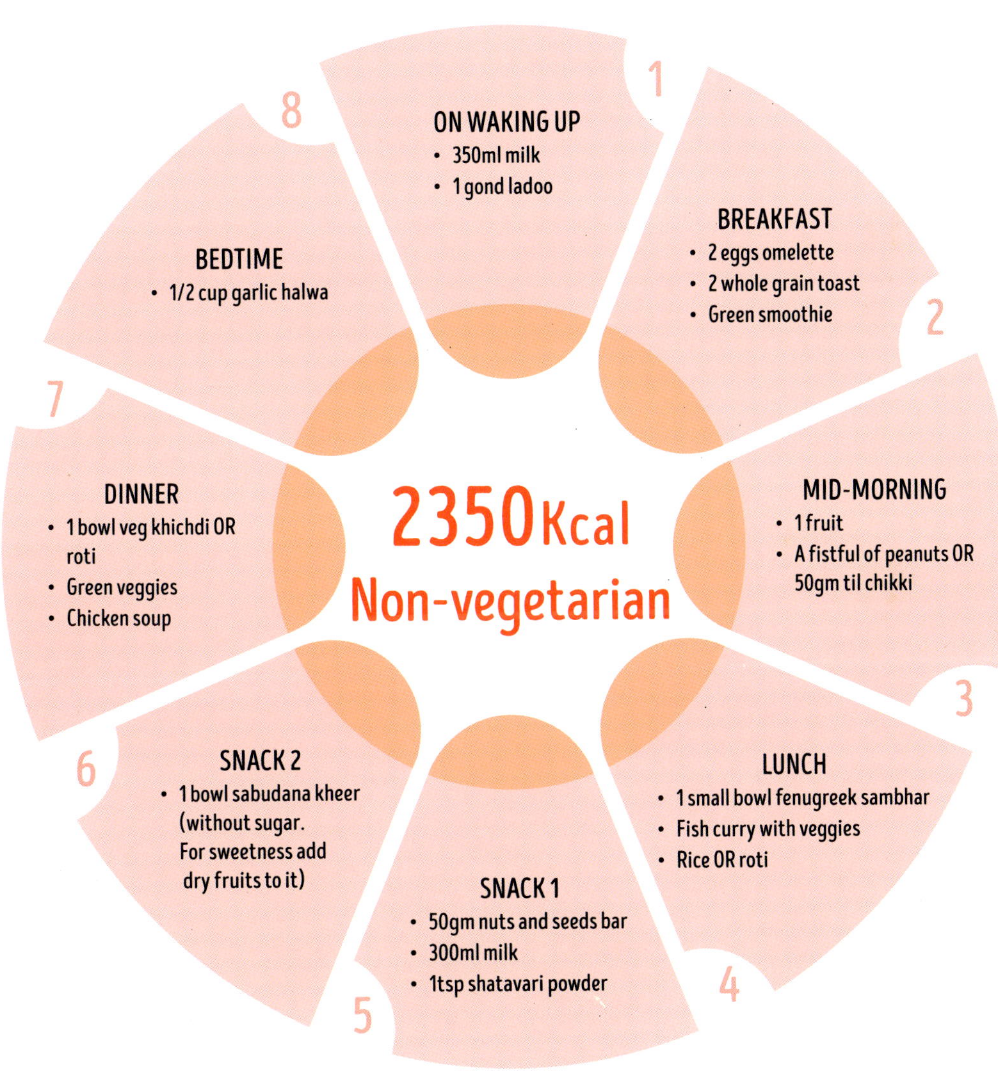

NOTES

- Fenugreek and khaskhas ladoo recipe on page 55.
- The green smoothie has moringa, which is very helpful in increasing breast milk. The recipe is on page 177.
- Sabudhana kheer is on page 121.
- We recommend the use of garlic in any form, whether to be added to chutneys or dals or even as halwa, as is prepared in the state of Tamil Nadu. You can find the recipe on page 41.
- To increase the iron content of food, iron vessels and pans can be used to prepare the food.
- If you are lactose intolerant, then paneer can be replaced with soya paneer or tofu. Milk can be replaced with soyamilk or almond milk.
- If gluten intolerant, gluten-free flour mixes made of millet flours can be used.
- Those who have thyroid complaints, please consult your doctor before using soy products in your preparation.
- One teaspoon of prepared legiyam can be given first thing in the morning to a new mom.
- Kankari ajwain can be taken after meals to improve digestion. Recipe is on page 97.
- A herbal concoction of 1 teaspoon dill seeds and ¼ tsp of dry ginger powder boiled in 1 litre of water to be sipped throughout the day and is great for digestion.
- We suggest that if the serving size of the traditional preparations recommended are adhered to then they can easily become part of a nutritious meal plan.
- The additional calories recommended are 350 to 450 calories in the second and third trimester of pregnancy. During the post-partum period it is generally 350 in the first six months and 400 calories in the next six months (refer to Section 1). So one or two (if low-calorie options are chosen) traditional dishes can be included daily if the serving size recommended is adhered to. This way one can add some unique micronutrients in their everyday diet and blend the old and new seamlessly.
- The recommended serving sizes are in standard measure cups and spoons. A standard cup can usually hold 200 to 250ml depending on the viscosity.

RECIPE IDEAS

for pregnant women and

HEALTHY SNACK IDEAS

for lactating mothers

Proteins

Fats

Carbohydrates

Iron

B12
Vitamin B12

Folic Acid

Calcium

Manathakkali Keerai Kootu (Sunberry Leaf Dal)

Not many are aware that this variety of greens is a rich iron source. It is consumed widely in Tamil Nadu. Makes a very tasty side dish with rice.

220kcal

20.5mg

20 min.

1 cup

Ingredients

Manathakkali greens (Black nightshade)	100gm
Green gram (Moong dal)	20gm
Jeera	1tsp
Mustard seeds	½tsp
Red chilli, salt, asafoetida	1tsp
Coconut	2tsp
Oil	1tsp

Method

1. Cook the finely diced greens in water with salt.
2. Add the cooked green gram dal.
3. Make a paste of coconut, red chilli and jeera and add to the above mixture. Temper with mustard and asofetida.

Pan-roasted Chivda

Easy-to-make, anytime snack popular in Maharashtra.

220kcal

20.5mg

20 min.

2 cups

Ingredients

Rice flakes (poha)	45gm
Roasted Bengal gram	15gm
Roasted peanuts	15gm
Curry leaves	10 nos.
Mustard seeds	½tsp
Turmeric powder	½tsp
Salt	To taste
Asafoetida	A pinch
Citric acid	A pinch
Oil	3tsp
Sugar	1/2tsp

Method

1. In a thick-bottomed pan, heat the oil and allow the mustard to splutter. Add the curry leaves, asafoetida and turmeric powder.
2. Add the rice flakes and roast for 5-7 minutes, add the roasted Bengal gram, roasted peanuts, salt and sugar and roast for 3 more minutes.
3. Add the pinch of citric acid for the tangy taste.
4. Red rice poha also can be used for this preparation.

Sundakkai Kadalai Kozhambu

(Turkey Berry and Chickpeas in Gravy)

A sambhar variant with lots of goodness, goes well with idli, dosa and rice.

220kcal

11.7mg

15 min.
+ soaking time

2 cups

Ingredients

Boiled chickpeas	100gm
Turkey berries	20gm
Tamarind paste	1tsp
Sambhar masala powder	1tsp
Mustard seeds	1tsp
Asafoetida	¼tsp
Curry leaves	4 to 5
Oil	

For wet masala:

Fenugreek seeds	1tsp
Coconut scrapped	2tsp
Red chillies	3 nos.
Black gram dal/ white lentil (urad dal)	2tsp

Method

1. Boil the tamarind paste after diluting it with 1 cup water with sambhar powder in a vessel.
2. Add the boiled chickpeas and salt to it.
3. Grind the ingredients of the wet masala after sautéing in a teaspoon of oil.
4. Add the masala to the tamarind mixture and allow to cook together for 10 minutes.
5. Give a tempering of Turkey berries, mustard, curry leaves and asafoetida in a teaspoon of oil and add to the above dish and remove from the heat.
6. This goes well with plain rice or curd rice.

Millet Methi Pulao

A low glycaemic index preparation suitable for pregnant women with thyroid and insulin resistance issues.

390kcal

6.8mg

20 min.
+ soaking time

1½ cups

Ingredients

Cooked little millet/ foxtail millet (samaa/kangani)	1 cup
Black chickpeas, soaked and boiled	¼ cup
Green chilli	1
Ginger	1" pc.
Garlic	3 pods
Cinnamon	½" pc.
Cloves	2
Cardamom	2
Ghee	2tsp
Onion	1
Cashew nuts	4-5
Coconut milk	⅓ cup
Fenugreek leaves	½ cup

Method

1. Take 1 cup of cooked millet.
2. Grind green chillies, ginger, garlic, cinnamon, cloves and cardamom into a coarse paste.
3. In a pan, heat a teaspoon of ghee and add sliced onion and cashew nuts until golden brown and keep aside.
4. In the same pan, sauté the masala paste and add the washed methi leaves.
5. Add the millet to the above and add ¼ cup of coconut milk for flavour.
6. Cook covered for a few minutes and garnish with the onion and cashew nuts.

Cheese Omelette Toast

This breakfast classic is also an anytime meal.

220kcal

0.94μg

123.4μg

10 min.

1 omelette

Ingredients

Whole wheat bread	2 slices
Egg	1
Spinach	½ cup
Mushroom	50gm
Feta cheese	15gm
Sun-dried tomato	3tsp
Garlic	1tsp
Cow's milk	1tbsp
Basil and oregano herbs	1tsp
Salt and pepper	To taste
Olive oil	2tsp

Method

1. Beat the egg and add milk, salt, pepper and herbs in the batter.
2. Sauté the garlic, spinach, mushroom and sun-dried tomato with olive oil in a pan.
3. Add the beaten egg batter to the pan on top of the vegetables spreading evenly.
4. Close the pan with a lid to cook well.
5. Toast the bread and top it with omelette and cheese.

Kanji Vada (Green Gram Fritters in Broth)

A traditional Marwari dish with unsuspected goodness factors.

151kcal per vada

*

324µg

20 min. + 2-3 hrs. soaking + 24-48 hrs. fermentation

8 vadas

Ingredients

Green gram dal/ black gram dal (moong/urad)	250gm
Mustard seeds powdered	2tbsp
Chilli powder	1tsp
Salt	2tsp or as per taste
Coriander seeds	1tsp
Cumin seeds	½tsp
Fennel seeds	½tsp
Turmeric powder	½tsp
Water	1 litre
Oil for frying	

Method

1. Soak green gram dal for 2-3 hours and then strain and grind it in a mixer.
2. Beat the thick batter and add ¾ of salt, ½ of red chilli powder, coriander, cumin, fennel and turmeric to it.
3. Deep fry the batter in the shape of vada or pakori.
4. Boil water and let it cool.
5. Then add salt, mustard seeds powder, red chilli powder and add the fried vadas.
6. Store it in a glass container and let it stay in the sun for a day or two.
7. Taste the water and if it has gone sour then refrigerate it.

Instead of the vada, red carrots and beetroot pieces can be added to the water and kanji made the same way. Consume not more than once a week.

* Fermented foods are documented to have high vitamin B12 content. Levels not tested in fermented kanji in particular.

Fermented Rice Drink

This simple yet nutritious meal used to be the breakfast staple in south Indian households in the past decades and is served as breakfast to farmers heading to the fields in the morning even today.

150kcal	*	101µg	5 min. + overnight fermentation	2 cups

Ingredients

White/brown rice, cooked	1 cup
Curd	½ cup
Salt to taste	
Shallots, very finely sliced	1tsp
Green chilli (or as per taste)	¼ pc.

Method

1. Soak the cooked rice in 1.5 cup water and keep it covered overnight in room temperature.
2. In the morning, the fermented rice along with the water and the good bacteria is blended with curd and a small piece of green chilli in a mixer.
3. Salt is added as per taste and finely sliced shallots are added on top for flavour, crunch and garnish.
4. It can also be consumed in the semi-solid form, without blending, along with some pickle.

Author's Note *Consume not more than once or twice in a week.*

* Fermented foods are documented to have high vitamin B12 content. Levels not tested in fermented rice drink in particular.

Ragi Dosa with Vegetable Kurma

This combination is a marriage made in heaven combining the crispy ragi dosa with the mildly-spiced kurma.

378kcal

475mg

15-20 min.

2 dosas

Ingredients

For Dosa

Ragi flour	30gm
Semolina	10gm
Curd	20gm
Jeera	5gm
Green chillies; ginger, grated; asafoetida, salt	To taste
Drumstick leaves, chopped	20gm
Oil	5gm

For Kurma

Onion	20gm
Carrot	20gm
Potato	20gm
Poppy seeds	2tsp
Oil	5gm
Ginger, garlic, garam masala, salt	To taste
Coconut milk	25ml

Method

For Dosa

1. Make a batter of ragi in curd with water added for consistency.
2. Add all the other ingredients except semolina to it and let it soak for 30 minutes.
3. Add semolina to a cup of water and let it boil for 5 min. Allow to cool and add the slurry to the ragi dosa batter.
4. Make dosa as usual.

For Kurma

5. Make a paste of ginger, garlic, masala, poppy seeds.
6. Fry the onion, add the paste and fry for a minute.
7. Add the potato and carrot along with water and allow to cook together.
8. Add coconut milk and salt.

Aloo Poshto (Potatoes in Poppy Seed Gravy)

This Bengali staple is a calcium treasure house.

440kcal

549mg

15-20 min.

1 cup

Ingredients

Potato	200gm
Poppy seeds	2tbsp
Green chillies	2 nos.
Dry red chilly	1
Jeera	1tsp
Salt and turmeric	To taste
Sugar	½tsp
Mustard oil	1tsp

Method

1. Temper cumin seeds, dry red chilli in mustard oil.
2. Add the diced potatoes and stir till soft.
3. Add finely diced green chillies, salt, turmeric, sugar and poppy seed paste to it and cook till the potatoes are done.

Methi Thepla (Fenugreek Leaf Flatbread)

This common Gujarati preparation is an ideal lunchbox item.

263kcla per thepla

355mg per thepla

15-20 min.

2 theplas

Ingredients

Whole wheat flour	45gm
Fenugreek leaves	50gm
Sesame seeds	1tsp
Ajwain seeds	½tsp
Curd	1tbsp
Salt, chilli powder	To taste
Oil/ghee	1tsp

Method

1. Make a roti batter with all the ingredients and roll into thin parathas. Cook on the *tawa*, brushing with oil.

Almond Sesame Chikki

This anytime snack is filled with calcium.

340kcal

416mg

10 min. + 2 hrs. of cooling time

4 pcs.

Ingredients

Almonds (crushed)	15gm
Sesame seeds	25gm
Jaggery	25gm

Method

1. Make a thick syrup of jaggery by heating it.
2. Add the almonds and sesame seeds and coat them well with the thick slurry of jaggery.
3. Spread it evenly on a flat, clean and cool surface and allow to cool.

Lotus Stem Pepper Fry

This tasty, low-calorie dish is filled with calcium.

159kcal

498mg

10 min.

1 cup

Ingredients

Lotus stem cut into thin slices	100gm
Pepper powder	1tsp
Garlic finely cut	2tsp
Salt	To taste
Sesame seeds	2tsp
Soya sauce	1tsp
Honey	½tsp
Oil	2tsp
Spring onion greens	4tsp

Method

1. Shallow fry the lotus stem slices in oil with garlic, salt and pepper.
2. Add toasted sesame seeds.
3. Add soya sauce and honey.
4. Garnish with spring onion greens.

Diya had a busy schedule with her one-month-old son Aryan. The breastfeeding routine involved interrupted sleep and constant vigil on her part. She had to battle her food cravings in the middle of the night when everyone else was asleep. She could not get up and make something for herself. That's when her Kamla Aunty became her saviour, bringing her some healthy snacks, which Diya could dig into while feeding in the middle of the night or between meals!

It not only provided her the required nutrition, the ingredients in it helped her improve her lactation also.

Halim Oats Relish Balls

These tasty balls are rich in iron.
Garden cress seeds are considered a lactation aid.

 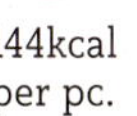 144kcal per pc.	17gm	4gm	8gm	15 min. + soaking time	5 balls

Ingredients

Semolina	¼ cup
Oats powder	¼ cup
Jaggery	¼ cup
Garden cress seeds (Halim)	¼ cup
Crushed nuts	¼ cup
Cow's ghee	1tbsp
Cardamom powder	½tsp

Method

1. Soak the garden cress seeds in ¼ cup of water in a deep bowl for 3 hours.
2. Heat the ghee in a deep non-stick pan, roast the semolina till it emanates fragrance.
3. Add the soaked garden cress seeds and jaggery, mix well and cook on a medium flame for 6 to 7 minutes or till the jaggery melts, while stirring continuously.
4. Add the crushed nuts and mix well and make small balls when slightly cool.

Green Smoothie

Superfoods in liquid form! Good as a lactation aid.

60kcal	11.5gm	1gm	1.25gm	2 min.	1 cup

Ingredients

Moringa powder	½tsp
Almond/Coconut milk	½ cup
Spinach	½ cup
Dates, deseeded	3-4
Chia seeds	1tsp

Method

1. Put all the ingredients in a mixer and blend.
2. Add water to get the required consistency.

Sattu Drink

This is a common drink among the Bihari and Marwari communities. Roasted Bengal gram powder (sattu) is a very rich source of protein, magnesium, calcium and folic acid.

100kcal	17gm	7gm	0.5gm	2 min.	1½ cups

Ingredients

Sattu	2tbsp
Water	250ml
Rock salt	To taste
Lemon juice	1tbsp

Method

1. Mix all the ingredients and stir well so that there are no lumps.

Nuts and Seeds Energy Bar

This delicious bar can be made at home with minimal effort. Ideal to carry as a snack to office or while travelling. There is no added sugar in this recipe.

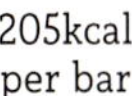

205kcal per bar

28gm

5gm

8gm

10 min. + 1 hr. refrigeration time

5 bars

Ingredients

Pumpkin seeds	½ cup
Sunflower seeds	½ cup
Coconut shavings	¼ cup
Sesame seeds	¼ cup
Flaxseeds	¼ cup
Almonds	¼ cup
Dates, deseeded	15 nos.
Coconut oil/Olive oil	⅓ cup
Cocoa powder	¼ cup
Vanilla essence	1tsp
Rolled oats	⅓ cup
Poppy seeds	2tbsp

Method

1. Place all the ingredients except oats and poppy seeds in a food processor, whizz a few times. Do not over process. Pour into a large mixing bowl.
2. Place dates, coconut oil/ olive oil and vanilla in food processor and blend until a smooth paste is formed. If it is too sticky, add a bit of hot water and blend until smooth.
3. Put this mixture over the dry mixture in the bowl and add oats and poppy seeds. Mix thoroughly. Use hands to mix well.
4. Spread it in a baking pan covered with plastic wrap. Press well evenly with wet hands or back of a buttered spoon.
5. Place it in the refrigerator for an hour to set. Cut into bars.

Peanut/Kabuli Channa Sundal

A fulfilling and balanced snack which is common in the southern states of India.

170kcal	18gm	7gm	8gm	20 min. + overnight soaking	1 cup

Ingredients

Peanut/Kabuli channa, soaked	1 bowl
Red chillies	2 to 3
Asafoetida	A pinch
Salt	To taste
Curry leaves	5/6 nos.
Coconut scrapings	1tsp
Mustard seeds	½tsp
Oil	1tsp

Method

1. Pressure cook the soaked peanuts or kabuli channa with some added salt.
2. Splutter mustard seeds, and add chillies, curry leaves and asafoetida in oil.
3. Add the boiled peanuts/channa to the above vessel.
4. Add salt as per taste and add coconut.

Savoury Seed Mix

An interesting savoury snack.

220kcal	25gm	5gm	12gm	5 min.	1 cup

Ingredients

Pumpkin seeds	2tbsp
Foxnuts	30gm
Cucumber seeds	2tbsp
Sun-dried tomato	1tbsp
Olive oil	1tsp
Mixed Italian herbs	To taste

Method

1. Roast all the seeds and mix all the ingredients.

Antioxidant Trail Mix

Calorie-dense, but packed with antioxidants.

 335kcal	36gm	8gm	18gm	2 min.	1½ cups

Ingredients

Almonds	¼ cup
Walnuts	¼ cup
Pumpkin seeds	¼ cup
Sunflower seeds	¼ cup
Raisins	¼ cup
Dried cranberries	¼ cup
Chocolate chips	¼ cup

Method

1. Mix all the ingredients and stir well so that no lumps are left.

A word about the recipes

- The recipes are wholesome and the ingredients create a balance when taken together.
- While using the quantity in the recipes, we urge you to adjust the ingredients. The serving size and amount of calories are given to help the reader make an informed choice.
- A person can choose to take three different low-calorie preparations with varied ingredients and properties or stick to one serving of one high calorie preparation.
- The amount of nutrients in the food will vary according to the variety, climate and region where the ingredients are grown.
- Please consult your doctor if you are on any treatment and medications before trying the recipes.

Some tips

- A handful of nuts and seeds can be also be had instead of nuts and seed bars.
- To improve the intake of iron, Malabar spinach or manathakkali greens can be added to any dal or chillas. Please refer to page number 151 for manathakkali keerai kootu recipe.
- Poha can be eaten for breakfast or a snack option. But make sure to add lime juice to enhance the iron absorption.
- A homemade elixir of iron for the vegetarians is the Turkey berry or sundakai, which is included in making angaaya podi (please refer to page number 43), which can be added to any of the vegetable dishes or dals, or can be had just with water. It will definitely boost the haemoglobin levels.
- To increase the calcium intake, poppy seeds can be added to any of the vegetables. Please also refer to page number 167 for aloo poshto recipe.
- Til chikki or laddoo made with jaggery is recommended daily or one can also add roasted sesame to the salad and veggies or to any of the chutney as it has a very neutral taste.
- For the folic acid requirements, spinach, mint or ladies finger can be included in the diet. Even sattu (roasted Bengal gram) is a good source of folic acid so the vegetarians can also include it in their meals in the form of stuffed sattu paratha or a sattu drink (please refer to page number 177).

Conclusion

Until about a generation or two before, eight children or an average of four children per family was a norm in India. This is common even today the rural areas where birth control is not practised. They managed pregnancy and childbirth with the help of only traditional foods and wisdom. Ingredients indigenous to the place were adapted into the regional cuisine, made into a local practice and also handed over to the next generation to follow.

Today, pregnancy is 'managed' by the 'mother and child' hospitals with all facilities, like dietician, birthing classes, pelvic floor exercises and expert lactation consultant, all under one roof. This is a convenient setting for the new-age mom. A few grandmothers who try to advise their daughters or daughters-in-law based on their experience get vetoed. They feel helpless trying to convince the younger women since they are unable to explain the significance or science behind their traditional logic and recipes.

This book attempts to unravel some of the oldest regional recipes of India for pregnancy and lactation. While collecting and reasoning the need for some ingredients, it was indeed surprising to know that most of the recipes were rich in micronutrients that's essential to meet the unique demands of pregnancy, postpartum and lactation.

The idea behind this book is to convince the modern-day woman about the conventional wisdom and offer her a variety of eclectic options from different regions of India, with sound scientific footing.

The authors firmly believe that this book will help create mass awareness about the hidden and treasured recipes of India.

About the Authors

Sonal Chowdhary

Sonal Chowdhary is a holistic nutrition consultant with specialization in weight management, sports and clinical nutrition. She is a certified holistic cancer coach from the Centre for Advancement in Cancer Education, Richboro, PA, USA. She is also an exercise prescriptionist from the American College of Sports Medicine-approved Exercise Science Academy.

She started off as an MBA graduate. The birth of her two kids and her passion for delicious, healthy food made her realize her true calling is to help people discover their incredible energy and achieve vibrant health. She takes an integrative approach to wellness, with a comprehensive focus on nutrition, emotional balance, and creates customized wellness plans for her clients to suit their lifestyles.

A yoga practitioner and an avid reader, she enjoys different cuisines and travel. She splits her time between Mumbai and Kolkata. You can find all the motivation and information you need on her website www.sonalchowdhary.com

Supriya Arun

Supriya Arun is a nutrition and wellness consultant certified in clinical weight management and sports nutrition. She is also certified in personal training from the American College of Sports Medicine. A postgraduate in pharmaceutical sciences, she spent eight years in the pharmaceutical research and development industry. She realized her passion for fitness and healthy eating when she started training and participating in half-marathons. An avid collector of recipes and cookbooks from across the world, she loves experimenting with modern as well as traditional cooking styles. Her husband and two kids are her willful guinea pigs.

She likes to travel and savour the local cuisines. She runs her own nutrition and wellness practice (www.heal-thy-living.co.in) where she combines her strong grasp of medical sciences developed over the years with fitness and food.

She believes that there are many ingredients that are hidden gems in our ancestral food practices waiting to be discovered. She also feels that we notice them only when the Western media talks about moringa as a super-food or the benefits of turmeric latte! It's time for India to start setting the health trends...

Acknowledgements

Writing a book was harder than we thought and more rewarding than we had ever imagined. The past year has been an exciting journey, from a spark of an idea to the actual book in our hands.

We would like to thank:

Our mothers, Sarita Bajaj and Vasantha Ramadas, whose encouragement, deep insights on the traditional practices and carefully collected heirloom recipes laid the foundation for the book.

Our husbands, Manish and Arun, who have been our respective pillars of strength.

Our children for being enthusiastic participants, tasting the preparations and giving honest opinions in book-related matters all along.

Urmilaji , Anjali Bhagat , Dayarani Sharma, Manju Joshi, Rashmi Rathore, Divya S.K, Mala Prabhu and Priya Pratap for sharing their household recipes.

Sucharita Vinod for testing two fish recipes in her kitchen and making them look photogenic.

Vinupa Sharma for her ideas and support.

Dr. Ashish Contractor, Dr. Vishwanath Prabhu, Krushmi Chheda, Kinita Kadakia, Disha Jhaveri Shah, Rekha Sudarsan and Chef Thomas Zacharias of Bombay Canteen for their special inputs and Bhavita Shah for all her efforts.

Dipti Patel (www.wordfamous.in) who believed in us and guided us all through the publication process.

Our designer Dhaivat Chhaya, who, apart from giving a tangible form to our ideas also helped us with photography tips.

The team at Jaico for their faith in the book and their vision.

All the members of our extended family, friends and mentors who have given us constructive feedback and their unconditional support.

Plus everyone else who have been part of this process but not mentioned above.

Bibliography

1. *Pregnancy to Parenthood* by Linda Golderg, Ginny Brinkley, Janice Kukar, Magna Publishing Co. Ltd.
2. *Williams' Basic Nutrition and Diet Therapy* by Staci Nix, Elselvier
3. *Nutrition during Pregnancy and Lactation* by Mitiam Erick
4. *Nutritive value of Indian foods* by C. Gopalan, B.V. Rama Sastri and S.C. Balasubramanian, National Institute of Nutrition
5. Does Insulin explain the relation between maternal obesity and poor lactation outcomes? An overview of the literature, *Advances in Nutrition, 7 (2), 2016; Laurie A Nommsen -Rivers.*
6. Systematic review of the efficacy of herbal galactagogues, *J of Human Lactation*, 2013; Mylove Mortel and Supriya D. Mehta.
7. The effect of naturally formulated galactagogue mix on breast milk production, prolactin level and short-term catch up of birth weight in the first week of life, *Intl J of health sciences and research*, 2014; Raji Srinivas, Kannan Eagappan, Sasikala Sasikumar.
8. Botanical Galactagogues, *Alternative and Complementary therapies*, 2008; Kathy Abascal and Eric Yarnell.
9. Common Herbs and foods used as Galactagogues, *Infant, Child and Adolescent Nutrition*; 2011, Frank J. Nice.
10. The effect of galactagogue herbal tea on breast milk production and short-term catch up of birth weight in the first week of life, *J. Alter Complement Med*, 2011; Turkyilmaz C, Onal E, Hirfanoglu IM et al.
11. Perspectives and attitudes of breastfeeding women using herbal galactagogues during breastfeeding: a qualitative study, *BMC Complementary and Alternative Medicine*, 2014; Tin Fei Sim, H Laetitia Hattingh and others.
12. Medicinal value of garlic: A review, *Intl J of Med. and Med. Sci*, 2013; Gebreselema Gebreyohannes and Mebrahtu Gebreyohan
13. Garlic: the science and therapeutic application of *Allium sativum* L and related species (2nd edition), Baltimore Williams and Wilkins, 1996; Hahn G, Koch HP, Lawson LD.
14. Effect of garlic on blood lipids in patients with coronary heart disease, *A. J. Clin. Nutr*, 1981; Bordia A
15. Garlic: A review of its medicinal effects and indicated active compounds, Phytomedicines of Europe: Chemistry and biological activity, ACS symposium series 691, 1998; Lawson LD
16. Garlic: A review of potential therapeutic effects, *Avicenna J of Phytomedicine*, 2013; Leyla Bayan, Peir Hossain Koulivand, Ali Gorji.
17. The effects of repeated exposure to garlic-flavoured milk on the nursling's behaviour, *Pediatric Research*, 1993; Julie A. Mennella and Gary K. Beaucahmp
18. The effect of naturally formulated Galactagogues Mix on breast milk production, prolactin level and short-term cach-up of birth weight in the first week of life, *Intl. J of Health Sciences and Res.*, 2014; Raji Srinivas, Kannan Eagappan, Sasikala Sasikumar
19. A double-blind randomised clinical trial for evaluation of galactagogue activity of *Asparagus racemosus* Willd., *Iranian J of Pharm.Res*, 2011; Mradu Gupta and Badri Shaw.
20. Randomised controlled trial of *Asparagus racemosus* (Shatavari) as lactogogue in lactational inadequacy, *Indian Pediatr.*,1996; Sharma S, Ramji S, Kumari S.
21. Systematic review of the efficacy of herbal Galactagogues, *J of Human Lactation*, 2013; Mylove Mortel and Supriya D.Mehta.
22. *Asparagus racemosus* (Shatavari): a versatile female tonic, Int J Pharm Biol Arch., 2011; Sharma K, Bhatnagar M.
23. Lactare for improving lactation, *Indian Practitioner*, 1986; Sholapurkar ML
24. Effect of *Asparagus racemosus* (Shatavari) on gastric emptying time in normal healthy volunteers. *J Postgrad Med*, 1990; Dalvi SS., Nadkarni PM, Gupta KC.
25. Identification of antioxidant compound from *Asparagus racemosus, Phytother. Res*, 2004; Wiboonpun N, Phuwapraisirisan P.
26. The Miracle tree: Moringa oleifera – Natural nutrition for the tropics, Church world service, Dakar, 1999

27. Moringa oleifera: A review of the medical evidence for it nutritional, therapeutic and prophylactic properties. Part1, Trees for life Journal, 2005; Jed W., Fahey Sc. D

28. Moringa oleifera "Mother's Best Friend", Intl J of Nutrition and Food Science, 2015; Egbuna Chukwuebuka

29. Moringa oleifera: A food plant with multiple medicinal uses, Phytother. Res, 2007; Anwar F, Latif S

30. Antioxidant properties of various solvent extracts of total phenolic constituents from three different agroclimactic origins of drumstick tree (Moringa oleifera) leaves, Journal of Agricultural and Food Chemistry, 2003; Siddhuraju P, and Becker K

31. Moringa oleifera as a Galactagogue, Breastfeeding medicine, 2014; Peter Francis N Ranguidin, Leonila F .Dans and Jacelie F. King

32. Effectiveness of natalac as a galactagogues, J Phil Med Assoc, 1996; Yabe-Almirante C, Lim M

33. Moringa oleifera as galactagogues for breastfeeding mothers: A systematic review and meta-analysis of randomised controlled trial, Phil J Pediatr, 2013; King J, Ranguindin P, Dans L.

34. A randomised controlled trial on the use of Malunggay (Moringa oleifera) for augmentation of the volume of breastmilk among mothers of term infants, Fil Fam Phys 2005; Espinosa-Kuo C.

35. A double blind, randomised controlled trial on the use of malunggay (Moringa oleifera) for augmentation of the volume of breastmilk amon non-nursing mothers of pre-term infants, Philipp J Pediatr, 2002; Estrella MCP, Mamtaring JBV et al.

36. *Anogeissus latifolia* -An Overview, *Res J of Pharmacognosy and Phytochemistry*, 2012; Ravi Dubey, Saba Sheikh, Vilasrao Kadam et al.

37. Hypolipidemic activity of gum ghatti of *Anogeissus latifolia*, Pharmacognosy Magazine, 2009; K.M. M Parvathi, C. K Ramesh.

38. Ethnobotany of Jalgaon District, Maharashtra, 2008; S. Pawar, D. A Patil.

39. *Anogeissus latifolia:* A Recent update on its chemistry and pharmacological application, *Pharmacology online, 2010;* Anudwipa Singh, Akhilesh Singh.

40. Antioxidant potential of *Anogeissus latifolia, Biol. Pharm. Bull, 2004;* R. Govindarajan, M.Vijaykumar et al.

41. Gum Ghatti: A promising polysaccharide for pharmaceutical applications, *Carbohydrate Polymers*, 2011; Anand S. Deshmukh, C. Mallikarjuna Setty et al.

42. Physiochemical properties of some Indian plant gums of commercial importance, Indian Institute of Natural resins and Gums, Ranchi, 2012; Dr. K.P Sao.

43. Phytochemistry and Pharmacological studies on *Solanum torvum* Swartz, *J. of Applied Pharmaceutical sciences*, 2013; Zubeida Yousaf, Ying Wang and others.

44. *Solanum torvum* Sw.-A Phytopharmacological review, *Der Pharmacia Lettre*, 2010; Ashok D. Agrawal, Puja S. Bajpei and others.

45. Immunomodulatory and eryhtropoietic effects of aqueous extract of the fruits of *Solanum torvum* Swartz (Solanaceae), *Pharmacognosy Res*, 2011; George A. Koffuor, Patrick Amoateng and Terrick A. Andey.

46. Antioxidant activity of commonly consumed plant foods of India: Contribution of their phenolic content, *Intl J of Food Science and Nutrition*, 2007; Saxena R, Venkaiah K et al.

47. Knowledge and use of forest product as traditional medicine: the case of the forest dwelling communities, Forest Research Institute of Malaysia, Kuala Lumpur, 1992; Shaari K, Kadir A.A

48. Ghana Herbal Pharmacopoeia, Ghana: Science and Technology Policy Research Institute, 2007.

49. Immunostimulant activity of dry fruits and plant materials used in Indian traditional medical system for mothers after child birth and invalids, *J Ethnopharmacol.*, 2000;Puri A, Sahai R, Singh KL et al.

50. Nutritive potential of a polyherbal preparation from some selected Ghanian Herbs, *J. Nat. Prod. Plant Resour.*, 2014; Rita Akosua Dickson, Isaac Kingsley Amponsah et al.